D

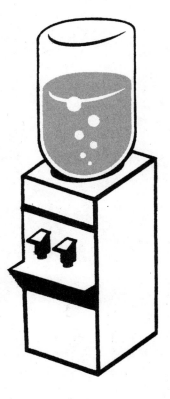

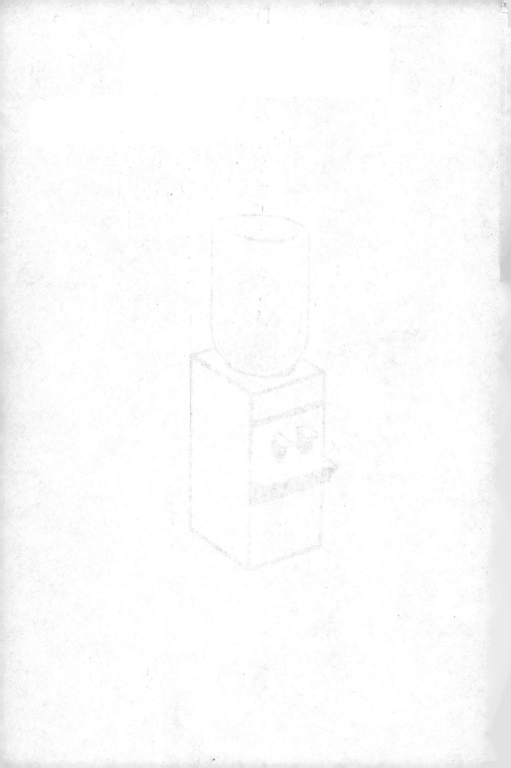

Should I Do What I Love?

Should I Do What I Love?

(or do what I do—so I can do what I love on the side)

Katy McColl

SASQUATCH BOOKS
SEATTLE

Printed in the United States of America
Published by Sasquatch Books
Distributed by Publishers Group West
10 09 08 07 06 05   8 7 6 5 4 3 2 1

Cover illustration: Kate Gebert / Croakandhum.com
Interior illustrations: Bob Suh
Book design: William Quinby
Author photo: Kate and Camilla Inc. / www.kateandcamilla.com

ISBN: 1-57061-457-1

Library of Congress Cataloging-in-Publication Data is available.

Sasquatch Books

119 South Main Street, Suite 400
Seattle, WA 98104
(206) 467-4300
www.sasquatchbooks.com
custserv@sasquatchbooks.com

Contents

Part II

The Aspiring Designer **41**

The Aspiring Director **63**

The Aspiring Gamer **83**

The Aspiring Political Operative **99**

The Aspiring Comedian 117

For Allison Conley

Acknowledgments

Thank you, David. Thank you, Erik and Laura. Thanks to Dick Todd, Vincent Ferraro, Nicomedes Suarez-Arauz, Nick DiGiovanni, and Larry Parnass. A huge thanks to Jane Pratt for giving me my dream job, and the most wonderful, entertaining, and inspiring staff at JANE.

Thank you, of course, to the most generous subjects and experts who shared their experiences in interviews. And to Camilla, Amanda, and Anne for their edits. To Heidi Lenze and the Sasquatch staff. And to Kerry Miller, who did all the work.

Introduction

I hope you like this book. I wanted to write something practical but also reassuring to people in their twenties who feel as though they're just starting out and already somewhat behind. Or those who'd like to get into an artistic career, but feel uncertain about where to start. I certainly didn't want anyone to have to slog through some humorless and esoteric treatise on why this period in life is such a tough one. I think it's pretty obvious. After swapping the no money but lots of free time lifestyle associated with being an undergraduate for the no money and no free time involved with answering someone else's telephone, you might be looking at your prospects five years into the unstructured expanse of Work that makes up "adult life" and be feeling rather discouraged.

On the other hand, this might be the first time you've really allowed yourself to look up. You may have spent years striving for the job you have now, only to realize that balance isn't easily achieved during two weeks of vacation a year. Theoretically, you're supposed to have a rough sense of whom you'd like to spend the rest of your life with. But as it stands, you feel disproportionately affected by Seasonal Affective Disorder. Oh, and you're broke. You may have changed your mind about this whole cubicle thing and want to go back to graduate school. Or any school, in fact, that will have you.

Personally, I love college students. I love lectures and workshops and natty college professors. But there are things that even the most well-intentioned advisors failed to tell you about what it was all going to be like once your occupation changed from Thinker to Drone.

In the spring semester of her senior year of college, my little sister met with her school's career guidance counselor. She asked him how to pursue a career in publishing, and he told her that the most important thing is to wear a suit to her interviews. Afterwards, he directed her to a database of what he said were the school's contacts in the publishing industry. In fact, it was just a list of each magazine's editor in chief. Their point person for *Vanity Fair* was Graydon Carter. And for *Vogue* it was Anna Wintour. The mere names of people running the show, which anyone can find on the masthead at the front of an issue, does not make for a very targeted list of contacts. Nor is it likely to yield many job interviews. And while a suit might be just the thing for someone who's applying for a job in banking, it tends to make applicants in the publishing field look somewhat less than cutting edge.

As a reporter, I'm responsible for becoming knowledgeable about subjects fast and have found that the best way to find things out is to ask someone on the inside. In addition to so generously sharing their advice and insights, the experts who have participated in this book describe how they got started in their careers. In some cases, they reveal how they pushed through their most difficult professional patches. Naturally, they aren't able to respond to every advice

Consider this volume your portable roster of informational interviews with some of America's greatest creative success stories.

seeker personally. So consider this volume your portable roster of informational interviews with some of America's greatest creative success stories.

As for choosing the subjects profiled in these chapters, I reviewed hundreds of stories from across the country, from a 29-year-old who's worked as a waitress, vegetarian chef, and dominatrix and doesn't know who would want to hire her because she's "barely educated in the Deep South" and has kids who are "sick half the winter," to one, who says, "All I've learned about the world since graduating college is that following your dreams means giving fake names at emergency medical clinics because you don't have health insurance."

Ultimately, I chose subjects whom I thought readers would be able to relate to. They're all struggling with what I would consider the typical problems associated with being in your twenties

> What induces a so-called quarterlife crisis is taking on jobs that are already out there, when the truly fulfilling trajectories are the ones you create for yourself.

and early thirties. Not one of them wants to know how to become a killer corporate counsel—not because law isn't interesting, but because we already know how to become lawyers. The more complicated question that the majority of interviewees want answered is how to make a living creating things, be it necklaces or performance troupes. They want to "start thinking again" and return to using their imaginations. They want to teach pilates.

It's worth noting that those who reported feeling the happiest and most fulfilled are either working for politicians they believe in or have left jet-set careers in order to become massage therapists. Through these conversations, I began to realize that what induces a so-called quarterlife crisis is taking on jobs that are already out there, when the truly fulfilling trajectories are the ones you create for yourself.

When You Don't Know
What You Want to Do

Not knowing what you want to do is like pumping gas in Montreal on New Year's Eve. It's the worst. Everyone around you is applying lipstick in their rearview mirror, en route to a party, wearing unseasonably skimpy sequined ensembles under big beaver coats while your hand cramps up as you clutch the high-octane nozzle. They're tossing cigarettes out the window capriciously—unconcerned about the 80 million gallons of gasoline stored under the convenience mart. These revelers don't give a damn. Their life has a sound track of good music, which you hear when they roll down the window just wide enough—literally—to squeeze out a Discover card. Your life's sound track, on the other hand, is cued to your customers' snow tires.

Don't Psych Yourself Out

It's cold in Montreal on New Year's Eve and you're this super-sweet, somewhat ambitious, thoroughly neato person who feels so beaten down by the Man and the Machine, you don't even care that gas station attendants don't earn tips.

First things first, don't psych yourself out. So you don't know what you want to do. I say, good for you. It would be really narrow-minded to formulate too laser-like a goal so early in life. Being open to what might come along or what opportunities you create for yourself is a wonderful quality. After all, part of real intelligence is acknowledging how much you don't know.

Try not to compare yourself to your peers, careerwise—don't let their immediate accomplishments discourage you from undertaking any project more ambitious than a nap.

Throughout life, you will have acquaintances who've known since their first trip to space camp that they wanted to be aeronautical engineers. And according to the Christmas letter/bragfest that their mothers send out each year, they are "just loving" their jobs at NASA. Let them have it. Let them bask in the conceit of decisiveness. I'm not trying to be mean. But rather to acknowledge that we are all bound to have crises—they just strike each of us at different times. Just because some friends know what path to pursue now doesn't mean their whole lives will be charmed. They might find out later that they feel pigeonholed. They might tire of the taste of space ice cream, if you will. So try not to compare yourself to your peers, careerwise. Because there will always be that prodigy freak show conducting an orchestra at 23 to devil you, or someone whose first novel is made into a blockbuster film. I don't want their immediate accomplishments to discourage you from undertaking any project more ambitious than a nap.

On a related note, you should feel proud of yourself for picking up this book. That's a positive, proactive score-one-for-you move because it means you want to make some changes. You obviously know you have enormous potential; after all, you could have picked up one of those self-flagellating "careers for dummies" titles instead.

Goals that Aren't Cheesy

Until recently, your life is likely to have been broken up into four- or five-year chunks. Many of the goals of these periods have been dictated to you by your parents, by your schools, and later, by your boss. Therefore, each step has felt more or less predetermined, with your work goals—(1) finish paper on "fragmented trajectories of individualism during the golden age of Spanish drama," (2) get internship, and (3) graduate—running concurrently with your personal ones—(1) hook up with bearded triathlete, (2) stop hooking up with bearded triathlete, and (3) quit using phrases like "fragmented trajectories of individualism" in breakup email drafts to bearded triathlete. And whether you've been canvassing for local politicians or enjoying the delicate fragrance of clove cigarettes and patchouli on freak street, all your life you've been building up experience and knowledge of the world and of yourself throughout all those painful, painful chunks.

It turns out, however, that you are not a person who wants to see your ass spread across the seat of an ergonomically correct office chair designed to maximize the efficiency with which you respond to emails during the next, say, 47 years. You have acquired that much self-knowledge, at least. So it's time to formulate new goals.

The people in this book who've gained traction in competitive fields tend to demonstrate how goal setting is the most effective, no-cost strategy for getting yourself out of or unstuck from any situation, mentally and professionally. It's particularly good if you're one of those contrary sorts because you set these goals for yourself, without any outside authority giving you flashbacks of PE teachers and chin-up bars.

In goal world, there's only you and what you want to accomplish. So I encourage you to make a list of where you want to be, in a big fat conceptual way (chopping onions in a kitchen with warm track lighting) or in specific places (at the headquarters of Texas Instruments). Divide your list so that the things you want to do everyday, like exercising or spending 30 minutes writing in the morning, don't get mixed in with the finite goals, like applying for a specific grant or running this year's Boston Marathon. Hang your list somewhere visible or attach it to your (nonhuman) coffeemaker with tape. That way, it will be in your face everyday, as opposed to something you peruse when you clean out the drawer of your bedside table.

Another good list to make has to do with the conditions under which you flourish. Some people really thrive on being in an environment where there's a lot of energy. They do their best work in a brainstorming, collaborating, risk-taking, positive-feedback-giving group. (Sounds a lot like San Francisco, doesn't it?) Other creative people think best in isolation, plodding away on a project until it's complete. Just because you're creative doesn't mean that you're a social creature. You might require the isolation of working at home because you can't deal with coworkers who say things like, "Somebody's got a case of the Mondays," and expect you to laugh.

Replacing Burnout with Creative Pursuits

Chances are, if you're feeling really clueless about your place in the world, it's possible that you've let yourself get distracted by the pace of everyday life. Or you're responding to crises as they arise instead of creating goals. In other words, you may be confused, but you're probably still really, really busy. Take Jennifer, 28, as an example. She writes, "I do some modeling, I bartend, I tried teaching dance for kids, being a receptionist at a hair salon, considered going to beauty school. I teach contact improvisation every so often when I can, and I feel like I am constantly trying to figure out what my perfect job could be. Or jobs. I do a lot of things, but none of them seems completely right. I fantasize a lot about other ways to make money [and] try to come up with get-rich-quick-type schemes to avoid thinking about what I really want to do day-to-day."

All that noise, that business, may prevent you from listening to all those deep, reflective parts of your psyche that know what really inspires you. You could continue in this vein for years, without any legitimate self-reflection, even if you do carry a sweaty yoga mat with you at all times. That's normal. Especially if you're burned-out. You may feel so burned-out that when someone asks you what you want to do, the most truthful answer you can muster is, "Quit." Or perhaps you're stuck at some sort of unfulfilling day job that sucks you so dry of creative energy that by the end of the day, even your eyelids complain of carpal tunnel.

If you're accustomed to short-term jobs, you're likely to balk at the idea of choosing a single-minded, one-track career path for all eternity. That, come to think of it, sounds about as stimulating as watching C-SPAN in an overheated room while wearing woolen tights and an ascot. You have well-founded reservations about that itchy ensemble, and you have well-founded reservations about signing up for any one career forever.

Stop thinking of your career that way. It's stressful. Way too much pressure to put on yourself and your blessedly nubile backside. Go back to living life in chunks. Try thinking about what you'd like to explore for the next three or four years. It may help to think about this naked—in the bath or while stretched out on something velvet. Have someone (dry) sit on a little stool next to the tub to take down your proclamations as they come to you. A natural editing process will kick in while generating ideas this way. And you can choose whomever you like to take dictation as long as it is not either of your parents.

How to Brainstorm

Feeling better? Or does looking over a list of interests that includes "making stuff" and "watching *Alias*" make you feel worse? That's OK. Bear in mind that not all the things you enjoy doing are going to be professional, moneymaking ventures. People in our parents' generation—i.e., people who stayed with the same company for much of their working lives—are always smarting off about how we expect too much fulfillment from our jobs.

Go back to living life in chunks. Think about what you'd like to explore for the next three or four years. It may help to think about this naked.

There's no reason to believe them yet. Instead, try to visualize your ideal work/life balance. Realistically, you might have to separate your hobbies from potential careers during this exercise, but this shouldn't have to come at the expense of satisfying your soul. In all fairness, we probably do expect too much happiness from our jobs. Then again, people from our parents' generation use canned cream-of-mushroom soup as sauce.

If you have a job that is woefully unfulfilling but pays you lots of money, make it part of a strategy. Don't up the fanciness of your "lifestyle" by quaffing rare, pheromone-infused cognac or outfitting your apartment with a jacuzzi and neon palm-tree lights à la *Coming to America*. Save it. Have all the money you don't need to live on automatically transferred from your checking account to an account that's stable but accessible in a jiffy, or any jiffy in which you decide to leave your soul-killing field and "do" Europe for a while. You'll regret it otherwise.

The only thing worse than feeling like a jackass is feeling perpetually trapped or enslaved by the so-called golden hand-cuffs. And when you do decide to walk away from your current job, you will at least have a cushion so you don't have to take a stopgap shift working as a barista.* A far more likely scenario, however, is that you have a job that's nonlucrative *and* unfulfilling, or you have no job at all. If this is you, take your mind off the spoiled whiner that the previous paragraph deals with and move on to the next.

Bear in mind that your priorities will change over time, based on what's going on in your life. You needn't think long-term in the traditional sense of the word, but it's always a good idea to consider what meaningful work means to you, because meaningful work tends to compensate for bad days and will keep you more satisfied over time. You may start out with Making a Shitload of Money as a priority, and that ideal later could morph into A 9 to 5 Thing That Enables Me to Veg Out and Read Comic Books While Answering Someone Else's Phone. Or maybe you want a job where you're not learning that much, but what you do is useful to someone and they allow you to Work From Home.

After four years of making visual and verbal presentations, for example, you might enjoy something—anything—that

---

*A word about being a barista: Few jobs help clarify your thinking and your ambitions better than this one. After dealing with enough grouchy moms and "touch of milk" types, you are likely to hit upon an escape route. What you fantasize about doing in your free time—away from people who correct your pronunciation of *biscotti*—is what you might consider doing full-time. Also, this is the perfect time to do those things and take those classes you never had time for in your pre-barista days. If you want to temporarily sell out by working at one of those global coffee chains, you can always transfer to a storefront in another country. Because if you are feeling hapless and aimless and, in all ways, less, what better place to be than Paris, which has a long and storied history as a place to suffer *la petite crise*?

allows you to work with your hands. Just know that it's easier to be poor and struggling when you're younger because your friends are likely to be poor and struggling, too. Together you can make a game of being craftily penurious—the Starving Artists' Alliance!—instead of having to stress out alone about whether or not you can afford to join your friends at restaurants.

During the brainstorming phase, it's OK to have a little vino buzz. It's OK to be impractical. You can (and probably will) choose more than one thing to do with yourself as an adult. Once you've settled on some things that excite you, you can start to really evaluate where your

The only thing worse than feeling like a jackass is feeling perpetually trapped or enslaved by the so-called golden handcuffs.

talents lie and which pursuits will sustain your interest for a few years. Ideally, there will be themes—overlapping or recurring fields of interest. And if there aren't, nobody's going to die here. You should just choose one or two areas to start with.

Exhaust Yourself with Research

The next phase involves a heck of a lot of research. You can stay in the bathtub for this section, but frankly, it will go a lot faster online and at the library. Start reading all about the industry or industries that you've earmarked, even if what you're research-ing is "jam" and you don't think of that as a full-fledged field but rather the cottage industry of nuns. Be not daunted, ho! Study up on the history of what you're interested in, what and who have come before you, any relevant legislation, the com-mon pitfalls, and the gossip.

If your interest is piqued by all this research, you are ready to move on to the next phase, where you get to visit a real live workplace and everything. It might sound a little scary, but you're about to send a letter (and then make a call) to two or three lumi-naries in whatever field it is that you've alighted on, asking if you can shadow them for a day.

Everyone loves a sycophant.

The shadowing concept has the unique advantage of getting you face-to-face with someone whom you can really learn from without the blatant Give Me a Job! over-tones associated with asking for an informational inter-view. It's the difference between being curious about them and demanding they be interested in you. Plus, if you follow someone around for a few hours, they'll show you what they actually do, as opposed to describing their work with abstract concepts like "team building" or "business development." And you'll spend more time together than if you'd stopped by all nervous-like for an interview, which will work to your advantage in a big way if you and Hotshot hit it off.

One more thing, don't be afraid to tell someone (if you're sincere) how much you admire their work and to ask point-blank whether you can shadow them for the day. Everyone loves a sycophant. And people like the warm, do-gooding feeling they get from showing a young person the ropes. You might not be able to get to Donald Trump this way, but you will be surprised who's within your reach. I have a friend who, during college, asked Robert DeNiro to come to campus to speak to students who were really interested in acting. Mr. DeNiro said yes.

If at the end of your research exercise, however, you realize that jam, or forestry, or high-endurance sea faring isn't for you, you'll have to recast of course. But don't lose heart. Research is a low-risk venture. It's free, for one thing. And for another, it teaches you a lot more than you would have learned while watching reruns of *Friends*. Win or lose, you will have more interesting tidbits to offer at cocktail parties or wherever it is that you choose to stand around smiling. As far as goals go, this one's noble and it will pay dividends in the end. Promise.

Steer Clear of Grad-School Escapism

After a number of long days at the library (including impromptu lunches from the vending machine), you will certainly feel fatigued. Your cuticles will feel raggedy and dry from all that page turning and coated in orange powder from the Cheetos. And your back might very well be hunched over and crumpled from too many hours spent perusing Google News. Now is a better time than ever to take a nap or even plunge your fists into a moisturizing tub of Crisco. Do whatever it takes to get yourself to settle down a little because you may be entering the danger zone where you're particularly susceptible to fantasies about going back to school.

Just to be clear, killing time in grad school is not a good idea. Yet it is the most seductive false idyll around. A lot of really smart people, upon finding themselves mentally under-stimulated or frustrated by the confines of the plebeian working world, go back to school for 3, 6, or 19 years to get an advanced degree in *something*. This can be a very rewarding life if you are a super-moneyed count or duchess of some sort. But it's a crummy idea for the rest of us. Indeed, if you scratch the surface, you might find that many academics are surprisingly frustrated. (If you're interested, you can read their totally titillating, anonymous, first-person columns about catty office politics and the like in the *Chronicle of Higher Education*.) Their cattiness, though, might just be a by-product of their breathtakingly competitive job market. Getting tenure (or tenure-track positions) can be as aspirational as making a living as a rock star.

Killing time in grad school is not a good idea. Yet it is the most seductive false idyll around.

If you just want to learn something or you miss having really good discourse (and your current book club meetings invariably degenerate into an argument over what to read next), sign yourself up for a class or two and see how it goes before committing yourself full-time. You might, for instance, regret pursuing a law degree if you discover you actually prefer to have nothing to do with lawyers.

If you absolutely do not have enough time to enroll in a continuing-education course, there is another way to evaluate the viability of enrolling in grad school. Get your hands on a copy of the syllabus for one of the courses you'd be taking in pursuit of your advanced degree. Read everything listed, as well as books you think are related. If you feel energized, you might be on to something with this whole grad-school concept. Otherwise, hold off as long as you don't really know what you want to study (modern poetry could be fun!) and regard grad school only as an option for the truly hard core. Trust me, there are many more delicious ways to go into debt than running up a tab with the U.S. Department of Education.

Now, I don't want to be presumptuous, but if you've thought and thought and really let your mind wander—naked, as instructed, with a confidant close at hand—and there is still nothing that you want to do or are interested in doing for the next two years, I must bring up the perhaps rude but very, very real possibility that you are a depressed person. And, well, that sucks. On a variety of levels. But that needn't be the end of it. Don't go covering up every millimeter of your bedroom windows with black electrical tape. No need to change your vanity plates to EEYORE after that self-pitying donkey either. There are drugs for these things: sunlight, endorphins, St. John's Wort, and Paxil. There are all manners of self-destructive avenues to go down as well, but they might very well set you back a career chunk or two, as I'm sure you've been warned about ad nauseam by your parents. In this case, the blessed old folks are correct.

When You Don't Like What You Do but You're Too Old to Start at the Bottom—Again

Now that you're older, you might not have the same tolerance for ramen noodles and dollar movies. Or perhaps you have the great fortune of having a spouse or a child (or what feels like enough children to re-enact Hands Across America) who depend on you to earn a certain amount of money. They are supportive and they think you're just great, and more than anything they want you to be happy. But they love the little luxuries that come with you working at your current job, without which there might not be a place to live, places to vacation, or anything as frivolous as organic fruit. Granted, the family might be able to forgo their good strawberries, but if you were to do a show of hands (or tongues) at the dinner table for who'd be OK with you quitting your job to pursue your dream of being a potter, some of your nearest and dearest might have trouble saying sayonara to electricity and the modern convenience of toilets that flush. Even the ones who love you may burst into tears, crying, "Why do we have to become mole people just so you can throw pots?"

Making Transitions

When April, age 29, emailed me, "For seven years now, I have been saying I hate my job as a clinical data manager," but explained that she can't quit to try something new because she has a one-year-old daughter and is the family breadwinner, I knew straightaway that her problem could hardly be overcome by quiet reflection or spirited flashcards. Or a flippant response from me. So I called an executive and life coach, Deborah Brown-Volkman of Surpass Your Dreams, and laid out the details for her.

Deborah says that people don't "start over." Or at least, they shouldn't. The practical solution is to transition from one field to another by blending the old career with the new. "It's very hard to say, 'I'm an executive and I want to be a clown,'" Deborah explains. "It's too big a leap for most people; they just can't handle that. So the goal is to take the skills that you have and transition." This can take a while and can eat up the majority of your nights and weekends, but it's a way of doing something more in line with your interests without having to jump sans safety net.

If April wanted to become a writer, for example, she could offer to write articles for publications that deal with her indus-try—in this case, the clinical-data world—as a start. You might be thinking that isn't the sexi- est thing in the world. And you would be correct. But transitioning involves being incremental and methodical in approach. And for some rea- son it's often easier to get a job when you already have a job.

After accumulating some bylines in trade publications, April could try writing for laypeople, translating some of the current issues in the clinical-data field that are rel- evant to everyday consumers into plain old English. April should be able to leverage her

Our ability to transition from one field to another is not a matter of knowledge or training but of resolve.

specialized knowledge — by virtue of working at her miserable job for the past few years, she knows so much more about this particular area than, say, a general assignment newspaper reporter ever would. She's an insider. She's an expert. And she probably knows a good bit more about a number of other specialized areas too. To follow Deborah Brown-Volkman's model, she should just keep building and expanding her level of expertise, starting with clinical data and branching out from there — until she reaches something that really interests her.

My friend Kate's mom is doing just that. She writes essays about the mental health industry and publishes them in medi- cal journals. Recently, she was added to the syllabus of a local university and is getting closer to publishing her more cre- ative stuff. In many ways, our ability to transition from one field to another is not a matter of knowledge or training but of resolve.

We are all insiders of something, whether it's a government agency or a restaurant violating a whole host of health codes. So when you're thinking about transitioning, try to imagine what kind of lines would need to be drawn between what you're doing now and what you want to be doing. It's like six degrees of separation; it's just a matter of identifying the degrees.

Re-establishing Happiness at Your Current Job

If you work at a large company, you really are in luck. First of all, you might be able to move to a different department. As a general rule, companies tend to be more interested in investing in their current employees than searching for new ones.

Even if you stay put, re-establishing happiness there might be a matter of changing your responsibilities—delegating the tasks that no longer interest you and asking for more responsibility in other areas. But the real appeal of the large company is that there might be opportunities for you to relocate to an office in another state, or

Variety and geography shouldn't be underestimated as factors in how you feel about your job.

for that matter, another country. Which means that you'd get to move and explore a new place without having to crash on someone's couch for a month.

Seriously, variety and geography shouldn't be underestimated as factors in how you feel about your job. Sometimes it's not even the work that you want to escape from but the work environment or the sameness of it all. You might feel underappreciated. Frankly, these are all sound enough reasons to get out of Dodge.

Try Something on the Side

Now if April told me that she wanted to do something totally unrelated, like making lamps, I would encourage her to take a slightly different approach. To that end, she would still need to carve out time for her craft on the weekends and at night and during her lunch hour. Setting boundaries is more easily said than done (in fact, everything is more easily said than done). But you must really endeavor to defend your creative time from other responsibilities. Like exercise, it has a way of getting squeezed from schedules when you're pressed for time.

April should also treat her coworkers as her client base and, at least initially, as an in-house focus group. How do they respond to the different styles she tries out? How much do they and would they spend on a lamp for themselves or as a gift? She should take their orders and commissions with the intention of growing her client base from there. This sounds pretty dry, admittedly. But the process itself of shifting your focus from the job that you despise to developing a side business can be completely energizing.

If the lack of deadlines associated with a low-risk side business almost seems to encourage your procrastination, find a partner. Not someone to make lamps with, necessarily, but a person who also wants to keep track of set goals and deadlines. A partner will hold you accountable for the progress of your chandeliers. Not to dwell on exercise metaphors, but it's a similar concept to having a workout buddy. Having a fulfilling and inspiring project on the side could—get this—even make you feel grateful for your current job and how it enables you to pursue your real interest in a low-risk way.

Now Might Be a Good Time for That Much-Needed Sabbatical

A more dramatic option (which I realize is not available to everyone) is to ask for a temporary leave of absence from your current position. It might sound crazy, but depending on a whole bunch of factors—how integral you are to day-to-day operations, how difficult you are to replace, how much specialized or sensitive information you're privy to, and how much training you needed to get to where you are now—it might be more advantageous for your employer to scrape by in your absence than to search for a replacement.

Of course, this might be hard to pull off if your current job is a highly coveted one. A line of wannabes from here to St. Petersburg would be willing to step in for any VJ spot on MTV, should you wish to have two months of "me time" in Baja California.

Then again, if your boss loves you and would do pretty much anything to avoid having to wade through 80,000 audition videotapes of aspiring replacements, the two of you may be able to work something out. People go on maternity and family leave all the time. Although, just to be clear, I am not advocating faking a pregnancy. That sounds unnecessarily complicated and sitcom-like. I think you would find this kind of shenanigan difficult to pull off without getting caught—and embarrassing to discuss with HR if you did.

When determining how much time off to request, it might be helpful to visualize a sliding scale. If you're making the coffee, three weeks may be a stretch. But your company may be willing to hire a temp during that time. If you're a vice president, you may be able to command a couple of months off. This is another situation in which working for a large company works to your benefit.

Another possibility is to ask for a reduction in hours or if you're on the road a lot, a temporary reduction in business trips. As long as you can basically keep it together, your manager should be humane enough to allow for a short period of time in which you're working 30 hours a week.

The bottom line is that there's no harm in asking for a leave of absence to pursue other projects if that's what you really want. Just don't tell your company why you're taking off. It's irrelevant and it's "personal." If your boss says no, you're just back where you started. It's highly unlikely that you'll give up any turf just for asking. Just make sure that you do so only after you really have a working outline of what you're going to do once you have some time off so that you don't while away the days scouring eBay. Internships and community-college classes are great places to start, but in truth, those are avenues that can also be explored without taking a leave of absence.

One more thing: Even if it's just in a cursory way, stay in touch with your office while you're out so that they don't forget how wonderful and irreplaceable you are.

Basic Schmoozing

You're going to have to do a lot of it if you plan on transitioning into a new career, so let's just get it out of the way: Networking is a great concept with a horrible, horrible name. It sounds like a gauche and greedy pastime when in fact, networking is just a wonky synonym for Charming the Pants Off People. If you're looking to make a radical or not-so-radical career shift, you should start networking right now so that you get to know as many people as possible in the field where you want to be. This, like all the tough situations in life, will require some brainstorming.

Let's say you're interested in leaving behind your life as a middle-school teacher and really want a job in the arts. You could cold-call the curator of a local museum and ask for an informational interview, but you might have more success if you introduce yourself to the curator at a low-key event hosted by the museum and make a good impression while you're there. Once the curator begins to recognize you as a gallery regular, then you can call to ask for a meeting, mentioning where you met and what you talked about.

If you are really serious about your career change, get on all the mailing lists of every related group or organization in the area and show up for all their events. Do something for them before expecting them to make a concerted effort to help you. Offer to organize events and be certain to volunteer at them. A cheerful and capable volunteer will always make more of an impression than a resume, or even the schmoozer who introduces herself to the curator. A consistent volunteer will already be able to add the museum's name to her resume and will have honest contacts there. Bear in mind that hiring decisions are often made by mid-level employees, not the head honcho, so make nice with everyone, even the plebes running the coat check with you.

When you meet people, don't ever ask for a job. It's rude. Don't make, "And what do you do?" your opening question, either. That's rude too. Instead, aim to really make their acquaintance. Tell them what you admire about them and their work. Ask questions about their interests, and their relationship to whatever event the two of you are attending. Do not go on about yourself, your accomplishments, or your haircut, for lord's sake. You have all day long to be self-absorbed. This is your opportunity to charm the pants off someone who knows about a working world you want to penetrate.

Networking is just a wonky synonym for Charming the Pants Off People.

If you can stay relaxed throughout this brief conversation, your common interests and enthusiasm will keep it from having a smarmy networking edge, and you won't have to work as hard to keep it moving. It all boils down to this: People like people who ask questions. And if you get people to talk about themselves, they will like you more. I'm not going to give you any hard-and-fast rules about being professional because sometimes being charming has more to do with being playful than being professional. And oftentimes being professional after hours is boring. So use your best judgment.

In general, it's best to meet people under the least contrived circumstances possible, like a PTA meeting or a concert. It's much more difficult to make inroads at career fairs where you're likely to be competing for attention with a lot of other job seekers. That would make me feel like I had to do something desperate or outrageous, and who wants to hire an arts administrator done up like a mime—with grease paint on her face and a T-shirt that says "Hire me and my heart will stop crying" anyway?

Fake the confidence you need.

If you're shy, don't panic. Shy people can make friends, too. All that's involved is saying your name and asking the person a question. Fake the confidence you need to do those two things and you'll make it through. No one, no matter how important or self-important, ever takes offense at people who introduce themselves. Later you can always send a little note with all the things you were "too shy" or "too starstruck" to say during your actual conversation, which is just about the most endearing note you could ever send. Except of course, "I've decided that I own too many vintage sports cars. Would you like to take one off my hands?"

In any case, practice making people warm to you in a short amount of time. You can try this by riding up and down the elevator of a random office building for an hour. Or, even more devious, you could sign up for one of those speed-dating events—not for the romantic possibilities, but because it will condition you to learn how to pique someone's interest in less than three minutes.

Learn Something New (On Deadline)

While you're brushing up on your charm, take a class or workshop so that you're developing some skill or experience. But choose your class wisely, based on what you want to get out of it. If you're honestly looking to make a career change, learn about your intended field, so that you're making progress as opposed to merely signing up for a diversion. If all you want is a good time after work, then by all means study faux marbleizing techniques.

Eleanora, 29, has never really felt like she had the freedom to pursue a creative career. As the only child of Russian-Jewish immigrant parents—"they came here for me!"—she's been working at Citibank for the past seven or eight years and taking classes in pottery and photography on the side. The trouble is, she needs to be in a class structured more like a boot camp—with deadlines and demands to combat her (very normal and very natural) professional inertia. As a vice president with her own office, she is "firmly entrenched in middle management." Every time she gets new business cards, she says, she gives half the box to her parents, who in turn proudly pass them out to all their friends. She's terrified of staying at the bank and "becoming one of the people I have nothing to say to at lunch."

Six months ago, Eleanora had the phone number of a career counselor sitting in her email inbox. She still hasn't gotten around to finding out whether her insurance will cover the counselor. "Should I do what I love, or do what I do so I can do what I love on the side?" she asks. "Do art on the side? Be a writer in the mornings? Is that really a way to be successful or happy?"

Maybe it's not the most exciting way to be happy, but it's what Eleanora needs to do, at least initially. It's almost tragic that the answer has to come in the form of patience and discipline because by the time that most of us gather up the nerve to actually do something, we want to do something drastic. Something histrionic even! Like snatching up our cartoon Cathy mug and firing off some salty language in the direction of our boss.

Resist this Hollywood bridge-burning scenario. You might need these people later, and they're more likely to support your next venture if they miss seeing you around and don't regard you as psycho. Unless Eleanora wants to take big risks on her own or freak the hell out of her parents, she should try something on the side.

How to Survive Being an Assistant

dmit it. You're way up near the 99th percentile of every standardized test ever administered to man, and you enjoy a well-rounded vocabulary and a coterie of wittier-than-average friends. Now you must convince someone that you want nothing more than to be responsible for answering their phone and tending to their filing needs. To be, in a word—and a rather vulgar one, in fact—their bitch.

Let's go there now: You're this bright young thing in some sort of plaid wool number, wielding a letter opener (the kind from Office Depot—not one of those endlessly elegant bone-handled daggers) and thinking, "I am a person of letters; I have the experience of a thousand internships. I'm better than this." Because, in truth, unless you feel genuine reverence for your boss, it's humiliating to pick up his or her dry cleaning.

Offer Yourself Up to the Big Cheese

If you're going to be an assistant, try to assist the most important person in the company that you can. Alternatively, you
can assist a high-up-ish person in the area that you're most
interested in, but try not to go down much further than that.
This way, you'll have built-in mentors where it counts, even
if they're not able to throw their weight around as effectively
as CEOs. It's like working on an assembly line that produces
stuffed dogs: You can share the workbench with the guy who
sews on the button noses. Or you can assist the foreman, the
one who supervises the fashioning together of all the doggie
parts—someone who really knows, and really cares, about
what goes on in multiple areas of the factory.

The truth is, there's nothing more demoralizing or unin-
spiring than doing menial tasks in a vacuum. Like making 500
copies of a document without understanding why everyone on
the third floor needs to read it
for the company to move forward. It's too abstract for you
to feel invested enough to
really hustle. A good boss, on
the other hand, gives you the
big picture: "We're trying to
sell more Christmas scarves
this year," or "Our mission
is to make trucker hats cool
again," or whatever the case
may be. A boss like this will
confer a sense of context and,
therefore, legitimacy to whatever it is that you're doing.

**Unless you feel
genuine reverence
for your boss, it's
humiliating to
pick up their dry
cleaning.**

Another benefit of working for the big cheese is that they know more than you do. They simply do; that's why they are too busy and too important to un-jam the fax machine. If you pay attention to them, you will learn some of what they know, which will eventually help you become more like them.

You're learning, by example, what you might be doing in 15 years if you stayed on this course—something you could never learn in school or from a website. You're also learning what kind of degrees and credentials people at the top have (and what it takes to get there). In addition, you're becoming privy to all kinds of industry culture and inside scoop. You're getting firsthand answers to questions like, "Is this world a nice environment, or is it catty and competitive?" and, "Do I even care?" After all, the pursuit of this kind of experience and know-how is the reason people take internships. If nothing else, this time you're getting paid.

> **You're learning, by example, what you might be doing in 15 years if you stayed on this course. . . and what it takes to get there.**

Befriend Other Underlings

You're likely to find a built-in set of confidants and allies in your fellow assistants. Make friends with them. Not only will

Choose your master wisely. You don't go around marrying people just because they propose.

they have entertaining abuse stories to share too, but they also will become your network one day.

When Chandra Czape started the website and networking group Ed2010, she says "it was about six or seven people getting together to talk about magazine jobs." There were no goals—just kids who were "all quite annoyed that you couldn't get jobs unless you knew somebody in the magazine industry." Her group focuses on the publishing industry, but the principle is the same no matter what your field. Essentially, the people involved in Ed2010 tell each other about available jobs. They also socialize. Chandra encourages new chapters to throw super-casual events where "people are literally sassing around a pub or a dive bar having a beer . . . you just don't feel comfortable when you're all straightlaced in some snooty environment with a martini in your hand." Four thousand people now subscribe to the group's newsletter, and her once small tête-à-tête has grown to encompass 20 city chapters and 26 college chapters.

Choose the Right Boss

When you're applying for assistant jobs, either through your network or cold, it's easy to get caught up in the idea that the important person at the other end of the desk is choosing you because they're the one conducting the interview. True, they won't be groveling or blowing their lunch money on letterpress thank-you notes, but you must still choose your master wisely. You don't go around marrying people just because they propose. As a general rule, try to avoid saddling yourself with any boss who uses the expression *think outside the box*—if for no other reason than it's doubtful that anyone who uses a cliché to describe creative thinking will be able to teach you very much.

You're probably thinking, "Damn it, Katy, I'm living at my parents'." Or, "I'm living in an apartment I can't afford, eating canned green beans. I'm dying here. I have no income and have to scrounge around for change to take to the Coinstar to buy lunch. I'm going to take the absolute first assistant job I'm offered, even if that means lying about it at cocktail parties." Believe me, I understand. Particularly if you're counting down the days until your student loans become due. But you have to honestly ask yourself, "Am I signing up for a year of doing menial tasks for some yahoo who won't teach me anything, or is a year of menial tasks the price of admission to breaking into a kickass career with a great mentor?" If it's the latter, you're in business.

Work Your Rolodex

When I first graduated from college, I was all set to become an inner-city Spanish teacher through Teach for America. Everyone I knew in the working world told me to "take advantage of this free time to explore, travel, and enjoy the good life," which I thought was pretty crummy advice to be giving someone with less than $100 in her checking account. (Plus the

$10 earned from selling back $400 worth of textbooks to the campus bookstore.) More than anything in the world—even more than being a teacher—I wanted to be a writer for JANE magazine. But since I had no idea how on earth a person went about getting a job in publishing, I was prepared to commit to a two-year teaching program so that I'd have somewhere to go upon leaving college.

Yet, I decided to at least go through the motions of applying for jobs in magazines. Like anyone with shaky self-esteem, I would send the resumes and make the calls, hoping that whomever I was calling wouldn't even pick up the phone so that I wouldn't have to endure opening with the painfully clunky, "I'm calling to follow up on the resume. . ." Just typing the phrase *follow up* makes me cringe with lameness. When I called JANE from my dorm room senior year, as nauseated as the first time I called a boy, they said quite literally, "Don't call us. We'll call you." At which point, I ran to the coffee shop to drink cappuccinos and smoke cigarettes with my friends and say mean things about the editors behind their backs. (Sorry!)

Just typing the phrase *follow up* makes me cringe with lameness.

Luckily, a super-cool editor I adored and had interned for at *Travel + Leisure* the previous summer sent around an email to her friends on my behalf when I graduated, asking for leads on job openings. I don't think I would have gotten a job otherwise.

But I did, one with an extraordinarily impressive and intimidating boss, who hired me in part because I said I was "a pleaser." I was thrilled. Furthermore, I vowed to make all decisions based not on fear, but with the intention of staving off regret.

Try to Be Grateful

During my first year of work out of college, mean people yelled at me. I was terrible at creating expense reports. If I got flustered, I would lose motor coordination and start bumping into walls. I cried. I made tons of mistakes. I suffered the effects of other people's mistakes. I misspelled important people's names. I hung up on people while trying to transfer their calls, and I drank too many saketinis at the ecumenical office holiday party. And yet, I was a pretty good assistant.

Trevor, 29, assists a man who refers to him as his "human coffee table." Which means that "when he wants me to take his cup away, he'll hold it out and call, 'Human Coffee Table!' He's a funny guy, so I don't think he means anything by it," but Trevor can't keep up this kind of subservience forever. In fact, if Trevor has to take "another assistant job for some rich bastard who doesn't 'get it,'" he'll "shoot up the place." Carrie, who works in fashion, says that her family simply does not understand that she's not allowed to take a lunch hour or receive personal phone calls: "Laypeople outside of the business say, 'Well, by law you're entitled, for every four hours of work, a 15-minute break.'" She pauses. "Those rules do not apply here."

My mother used to say that I wasn't getting paid enough for me to even think about my job at night and weekends. In fact, I kept a spiral notebook next to my bed so that I could

> It was only in working for a much smarter person that I was able to cotton on to why I was starting at the bottom and how much I needed to learn in order to move up.

write to-do lists when I woke up anxiously in the middle of the night. But the way that I was compensated did not manifest itself in my $700 biweekly check. I was earning the respect of a mentor. And it was only in working for a much smarter person that I was able to cotton on to why I was starting at the bottom and how much I needed to learn in order to move up.

Maybe ass-kissing doesn't come so easily to you. If this is the case, it's even more important that you really respect the people whose travel plans you're arranging. Because if you don't want to become them one day, you're sucking up to the wrong person. And that puts you at risk of burning bridges. Except under the most extenuating of extenuating circumstances, never, ever, ever leave a job on bad terms. Because then you'll lose the reference, which is part of why you're doing the job in the first place. "Every time I wanted to stab my first boss with a letter opener," says Anne, who was an assistant at a nonprofit in Philadelphia, "I thought, 'I could do that or I could have his signature on a letter.'"

When You Love Your Job but Can't Afford to Live on Your Salary

I write this chapter as I write many chapters, thinking about my friend Mary, who was so poor while job hunting that she would eat salad dressing for dinner. And drink Gatorade for lunch. She used to confide in me that while she was drinking her Gatorade, she would imagine how good she'd look in the black cashmere turtleneck she saw in the window of Barneys because being strapped was making her positively Hepburn-esque. She went on sixteen interviews over the course of more than a year. She had solid references and a couple of connections to boot. In many instances, she had marvelous chemistry with the people conducting her interviews. But she wasn't getting any offers. Eventually, she started to inquire, after being passed over for the 10th time, what exactly was wrong with her. The answers were as useless as they were maddening: underqualified, overqualified, too outgoing, not outgoing enough, and so on.

As it happens, there is nothing wrong with Mary, and she ultimately landed her dream job (for now) at the crème de la crème of ooh-la-la fashion houses. Two years later Mary can go to a bar and actually order something, amen. But she continues to hold on to her part-time job selling clothes at a chain store—where they have her take out the trash at the end of her shift—because she's so afraid of ever being that broke again.

Debt Is a Four-Letter Word

First off, you probably would rather not have this pointed out to you, but you could do worse than to love a job that isn't lucrative. You could hate your job and your whole profession. "Every woman I've ever worked for has a cat and is alone and miserable," says Carrie, 32. "The minute I got my cat I was like, 'This just seals the deal!'"

That said, you've got to stay afloat somehow. When I first started working, I drove myself deep into debt. Not because I was living high on the hog or anything, but because I was living beyond my means. Instead of moving into a one-bedroom apartment with one other girl, I should have taken a page from the women I interviewed while researching this book who shared one-room studio apartments with their

I had what might be called credit-card issues.

friends as a cost-cutting measure. That includes the bed. But I wasn't that resourceful, so I ended up bouncing checks—not all the time, but enough to seem flaky. Like Carrie, I had what might be called credit-card issues. "My first salary was $16,000 a year," Carrie says. "My family would be like, 'Why are you $40,000 in credit-card debt?' But it was because if I wanted to buy tampons, I would have to charge them."

In any case, when my roommate wisely quit New York for sunny California and an apartment she told me had "dual master suites," I moved in with my parents and commuted five hours every day. My older brother sat me down and discussed my budget with me. I'm surprised he was able to tolerate someone so delusional she gasped when he slashed her taxi fund. He insisted I set up automatic contributions to my 401(k)—that is, after explaining to me what one is. Basically, he rescued me. After a few months I was back in the black, and I never went back to taxis.

If you don't have a big brother or someone who can sit down with you to make a budget, visit a financial planner. They have all kinds of resources. Also, don't let embarrassment over your current financial outlook (or the fact that you've never balanced your checkbook) impede you. No matter how bad you think your situation is, I assure you they've seen worse. And many of these planners are free. (You can search for a reputable one at www.napfa. org or www.cfp.net.)

You could do worse than to love a job that isn't lucrative.

The Inevitable Second Job

My point is that there are three strategies for people who love the gig but can't live on it: cutting back, earning more, and managing your money more wisely. Earning more can mean supplementing your job like Mary did with part-time work in another field. It can mean doing freelance work that's very similar to your full-time gig. Or it can mean selling empanadas at Phil Lesh concerts and having a craft table at street fairs. Most of us take supplementary work at one time or another: catering, serving cocktails, crafting, copyediting, or stocking shelves during the Christmas rush at Barnes & Noble.

Pitiful as it is, unless you're working in one of those high-paying finance jobs, it may take a few promotions to get a decent living wage. But that's all the more reason to stick out your current job until your money struggles become less dire and you can turn your attention to your other problems. Seriously, it's good for your overall self-esteem to know that you can earn extra money when you need it.

There are three strategies for people who love the gig but can't live on it: cutting back, earning more, and managing your money more wisely.

Your Personal Budget Cuts

If you feel super-possessive of your downtime and can't bear the thought of cutting it in half, take aim at your current expenditures. First, can you reduce your monthly overhead-by getting a cheaper apartment, a cheaper car, and lower interest rates on everything? Can you order brewed coffee instead of lattes? Purchase your cigarettes over the internet, or better yet, quit? Do you have a taxi problem like I did? Are you ordering top-shelf liquor instead of Popov at bars that make you pay a premium for "ambience"? Using the treadmill at the fancy gym instead of the YMCA? I don't want you to have a joyless life without any pleasures. But I also want you to be solvent.

The Banal Money-Managing Section

Managing your money is kind of the boring stuff that I was hoping you'd pawn off on your own brother or your financial planner, but here are some of the basics. In addition to zero-interest student loans, the most important element in saving money is how early you do it, not how much you save. Even if you have only $50 drafted from your checking account each month into a high-yield savings acccount, you'll be working towards a more stable financial position. And if the transfer is automatic, you really won't feel it as much as if you had to write a check.

Speaking of checks, you must sign up for overdraft protection. One of the more unfair things about a bounced check is how much it costs you in penalties. With overdraft, this will no longer be a problem. As an aside, if you call your bank and give them a reasonable enough excuse for why your check bounced, they'll often refund those (bogus, if you think about it) charges. In which case, banks are the best!

Extreme Thrifting

I hesitate to share too many of the extreme options of economizing. But what the heck—here goes: One brilliant 27-year-old drone I interviewed revealed to me that she would often scoop the leftover Danish that are discarded in the trash of the office kitchenette after meetings and eat them for breakfast herself.

Don't drink away your paycheck.

If that's too fabulous to consider, start cooking. Cooking is always cheaper than eating at T.G.I. Friday's. Whipping up your own meals, however, involves a certain amount of planning ahead; if you don't have groceries, you'll end up eating out every meal anyway. Also, I hate to admit it, but going vegetarian (and by that I mean eating primarily vegetables, not imitation meats) is one of the cheapest options of all.

Here's another boring but chic cash-saving tip: When outfitting yourself, buy black, tan, and navy clothes so that everything in your closet will go together. Shop at charity stores located in fancy neighborhoods. One woman's closet absolution equals your scoring Armani pants. Master the domestic arts of mending your own buttons and growing your own plants. Finally, don't drink away your paycheck. Spending $30 a week on alcohol isn't really the act of someone who's making the tough cuts. I know it's cruel, and I'm sorry, but you might have to start picking people up in retro places like the Laundromat instead for the long-term benefit of your wallet.

The Aspiring Designer

ometimes at night, I yell at Star Jones," says Sydney, 28. She's sitting on the floor of the railroad apartment she shares with her boyfriend in Brooklyn surrounded by tissuey pattern paper (which I like) and very sharp pencils (which strike me as dangerous). Sydney's a fashion designer—I don't want to use the word *struggling* because she makes inspired clothes that are sold in three boutiques in New York—but in some ways, she's in a bad way. She tells me she's had four runway shows, counting "the shitty bar ones during fashion week," but not counting "the shitty bar ones that weren't during fashion week," including the nautically themed show, "Pirates vs. Sailors Fall 2004."

However, she's a secretary three days a week and can't afford to buy fabric to make her next collection. No benefactors or rich relations in sight. "On top of that," she says, "my ukulele band released a single in the U.K. called 'My Gay

Boyfriend' and is starting to get radio play in the U.S.—the band is really fun, but no money there, either. It's your average 'I want to be a designer, but instead I'm a poor, novelty-pop star/secretary' dilemma."

Clearly, this is a talented and multifaceted individual we're dealing with—not just some naive dreamer who scotch-tapes Calvin Klein underwear ads to her wall and Bedazzles belts made of tube socks.

It's your average "I want to be a designer, but instead I'm a poor, novelty-pop star/secretary" dilemma.

In any case, Sydney's been slogging away at this fashion stuff for a while. When she came to New York after grad-uating from Sarah Lawrence, she worked for an internet por-tal that catered to plus-sized women and as a costumer for off-off-Broadway theater pro-ductions. Naturally, she was laid off from the dotcom but was able to launch a small business as a fashion designer in the months she was on unemployment. (Only suckers, as it happens, use this brief respite to look for jobs.)

Sydney thought her fashion moment was upon her when she found out that one of her dresses, a darling red cotton wrap number that converts to a skirt, would be featured on *The View*, that unstructured, seemingly nine-hour television show featur-ing Barbara Walters, a couple of ninnies, and a whole lot of chit chat. All three boutiques that carry Sydney's designs ordered a bunch of the dresses and everyone Sydney knew tuned in to watch. Who could have known that Star Jones, who moon-lights as a shill for Payless ShoeSource, would cluck, 'Now, how much are you gonna charge for that?' before changing the subject.

Sydney was devastated. Which is why at night she's started having those crazy-person dialogues with Star Jones: "I ask her about slave labor and ask her how much she makes in an hour." The irony is that when Sydney was working at the plus-sized website, Star Jones had approached the portal about sending her and her friend on a $50,000 vacation to Africa, which she proposed she could write about afterwards. Perhaps that's nei-ther here nor there, but can you imagine?

The other rotten detail is that a gang of lady lunatics recently hit one of the co-op boutiques where Sydney sells her clothes and shoplifted a smattering of her most expensive handmade gowns. Poor Sydney's been in a funk ever since.

Perhaps the real issue, though, is that Sydney taught her-self how to sew by making costumes for the theater, and now she's competing for entry-level fashion house jobs with gradu-ates of design schools like the Fashion Institute of Technology (FIT) and Parsons. People with highfalutin credentials who will answer the phone for free.

"I would like to have health insurance and not be a secre-tary anymore, but I really want to make clothes," says Sydney, showing me a high-necked wool blouse with rusching. It's the kind of top a woman might pair with equestrian boots to pop down to the market to pick up a fresh baguette and some dai-sies. Understated, yet glamorous. Quite unlike Ms. Jones. "It's lonely being one girl with a room full of clothes and my sew-ing machine and no money to buy fabric," Sydney says.

Heatherette on Becoming a Sensation Without a Traditional Design Background

Heatherette is a design duo made up of Richie Rich and Traver Rains, nightclub icons who make really pretty fabrics and trim dresses with rick-rack, pom-poms, and feathers. Their designs are sold at Henri Bendel and Nordstrom. And their studio, a little pink workshop in the East Village, is full of fabrics and sequins and Hello Kitty graffiti on the walls. When they prepare for fashion week, they play cheesy romantic comedies like The Sweetest Thing *on the VCR. When Richie Rich yells out, "Interview time!" he and Traver take their places underneath a glittering turquoise chandelier, "a studio-warming gift from David LaChapelle." Richie does most of the talking. He wears a silk scarf tied around his head like Greta Garbo. It's entirely fetching.*

Richie: My launching pad was at nightclubs. The nightlife beckoned me in, and I met a kooky cast of characters in New York.

Traver: The people that we met kind of laid the groundwork for getting us off the ground.

Richie: We met Andy Warhol. We were creating these parties at nightclubs. So naturally, if you're going to have a party seven nights a week, you need something to wear. We spent all our money on shoes and made all our own clothing. And then I started making everybody's stuff. You know, everybody needs a vintage tuxedo jacket covered in like 5,000 spangled stars. A pair of leopard leggings. Glitter underwear was a big hit. There were a lot of friends around me that were aspiring fashion designers and a lot of the kids I was hanging out with were going to FIT and

Parsons. They were all going to school for fashion while I was going to the school of disco.

Traver: I came to New York with an open mind, not sure what exactly I was going to do. I have a degree in economics from Southern Methodist University. I didn't really get along on Wall Street so I ended up giving horseback-riding lessons at Chelsea Piers. That's where I met Richie.

Richie: I was in the Ice Capades and trained in figure skating all my life. I did a little ice skating at Chelsea Piers and my friend wanted to take horseback-riding lessons. Travor was the instructor. I was making my things that were kind of derived from the Ice Capades, with sequins. I started making T-shirts and was selling them at Patricia Field's, and Traver, with his degree in economics, said, "Well, you could have a clothing line, that way you wouldn't have to work in nightclubs." And I'm like, "If you want to do it with me, I'll do it, but I don't want to do a business on my own." Because I can make the stuff, but as far as getting it to the stores on time, forget about it.

Traver: We knew we don't have the schooling and all the technical abilities, so we had to focus on what we could do. But the thing that sets us apart from the other aspiring fashion designers is that we really took the connections that Richie had established and we just started calling editors.

Richie: Growing up, one of my hobbies was reading fashion magazines. We sat down and looked through all my favorite magazines and said, "Oh that's the editor! Let's call the editor!" Now I find that kind of funny, because all these people told us that we must have been really naive in a way because that's kind of not what you do. You usually have a showroom or something.

My motto is, "Don't ask, don't get."

Traver: Or we'd see someone out one night and they'd say, "Give me a call tomorrow." We'd definitely follow up on it.

Richie: [To] one girl, the fashion editor at *ym*, I said, "Can you come to our place?" And she said, "I'd rather have you come to my place." And I said, "Come to our place!" I always felt it was better for someone to see our environment. She saw our T-shirts and said, "Oh, they're great. You should do something [for us] sometime." And I said, "Can we do the cover?" My motto is, "Don't ask, don't get." And she kind of giggled and said, "Well, we are doing N*SYNC tomorrow." And so we stayed up all night and made 55 T-shirts. And we got the cover. Once you have one thing like that—it doesn't last long, but it gives you a little bit of leverage—to actually say you're doing something.

Traver: The first couple of collections, we worked so hard. I mean 24/7.

Richie: Traver and I were actually boyfriends at the time. I think we broke up because I went out every night because I felt like we needed to meet people. I'd already met half of New York, but I needed to meet the other half. It was fun, actually having a product that you were proud of and felt like it was going well. We also had a little band. And we had our names on our T-shirts in rhinestones. And Patricia Field [the costumer for *Sex and the City*] said, "Why don't you make that for Sarah Jessica Parker, for Carrie." So we made a Carrie T-shirt that ended up getting on all the worldwide billboards for *Sex and the City*. At the same time, we went to *Women's Wear Daily* because my friend said that's the bible of fashion. We brought over a garment bag and were basically like, "This is our stuff!" And they called Bridget Foley, the editor, down and she gave us the whole back page. That would be our break, I guess. I didn't really know why she did it. Maybe it's that whole downtown New York thing and she saw the eagerness in our eyes.

Traver: Keeping funding going the first year was a total struggle. We kept going out to little boutiques. We had no quality control. Shipping was a nightmare.

Richie: We had Bloomingdale's come over. They placed a $14,000 order for 4,500 shirts.

Traver: We were really lucky to get some good sponsorship for our shows.

Richie: We'd sit down and be like, "Coca-Cola sounds great." And then we'd call up some publicists. One called us back and said, "I represent Coca-Cola and I think you guys are fun." So that covered that. Call anybody and everybody. And always ask for the top person.

Richie: They see you as wacky and having fun, but I don't think they always necessarily realize that you're serious about it as well. So with the sponsors, we'd always really

Call anybody and everybody. And always ask for the top person.

have to song-and-dance them into understanding that we're not there to make a fool of anybody. We were there to respect their product but also there to get our job done, in a way. Because it's business.

Traver: Because of where we come from, we had the reputation as being from the club scene, East Village, underground, and all

of that. Corporate sponsorships kind of shy away from that. We had to prove to them that we were serious.

Richie: There's tons of money out there. It's just a matter of finding it. We have a good friend—a friend of a friend—who's a...an investment banker. And he came to one of our shows. And he's like, "What's going on? You guys should be everywhere." He found us two venture capitalists. It's taken us about 20 months. And we just now signed the deal, under a big group that actually backs different brands. A four-year deal.

> **You really have to make a niche of who you are and what your company is based upon. Explode that.**

Traver: It basically took a year of meetings, with different venture-capitalist people, to even find the right ones.

Traver: A lot of times it's torture, the struggle just to keep the collections going. Struggling to eat. Even now, we do not go out shopping for ourselves. We don't have any extra money. Anything extra, we put back into the business.

Richie: The other thing for a designer is you really have to make a niche of who you are and what your company is based upon. Explode that. In the beginning, when we were first starting out, the press started labeling us, "Trashy," "Club," "Nightlife," and at first I was like, "I don't want a niche; I don't want to be labeled." But I realized that everything gets a label. We're packaged as fun, these nightclub people. And at first I was like, "That's so boring and typical," but then I'm like, "Wait a minute. Not everybody was a club kid. Not everybody goes out." There are so many kids around the world who want to put on a party dress and kick up their heels once or twice. But we also make a fantastic pair of jeans. So it's a lifestyle that we've learned how to brand. But not even intentionally. Whether you're a musician or a fashion designer or what have you, it's like sexuality—they have to label you. They're going to say, "Are you a Ralph Lauren–type designer, a Betsey Johnson–type designer?" You don't have to compare yourself to these people. Focus on [promoting yourself] for a while. Help these people get to know you. When you're starting out, people will ask you, "Where do you sell? Where's your press?" You need one or the other. Try to get attention and try to get it out there. Get the buzz and the hype up. If you can't do both, concentrate on one and try to keep your head above water. The business people we're dealing with, they said, "You can't buy this kind of press." They tried to quantify it. They said we wasted $2 million in press. And we said, "Oh, no we're just getting started."

Jessica Naddaff on How to Be Your Own Publicist

As a vice president at Siren Public Relations, Jessica is one of those people for whom the expression "finger on the pulse" is trotted out. And as such, she's in charge of the campaigns for over 25 brands, including Urban Decay Cosmetics. She is also very young (27) and very smart (summa cum laude from Barnard!) and brings a tremendous amount of grace to the field of PR. *From time to time, she also gives me free samples.*

The first thing I would do is buy all the top magazines—all the fashion magazines—and rip out all of the mastheads. All the information you need is right in the masthead. It has the direct-dial number for every magazine. Find the name of the fashion editor, pick up the phone, and introduce yourself. Say, "Look, I have this great stuff. This celebrity wears it. It's already in this store. Can you come by?" Usually they'll go to [your] showroom or wherever you have your collection hanging up to come check it out. Or they'll send their assistant to check it out. That is probably the biggest and most important first step. Just reaching out. It's totally scary. But have it all together, all your selling points, any notable thing. Because they're always trying to find the latest, newest, coolest undiscovered talent.

In order to get in something like *Vogue*, there needs to be some sort of cachet. Either a celebrity or a socialite who's wearing it. If you've studied under [a famous designer] for a long time, like a protégé. Picking up the phone is honestly the best way to do it. Put together a look book. Send it to the editor with a letter. Then call and follow up. You should also call the local press and position yourself as this rising star. Definitely also get in touch with the fashion trade press. Literally, that is just picking up the magazine and looking to see who is writing the stories, calling the general number and getting transferred, and introducing yourself.

Sometimes our clients can get further if they call [reporters and editors] themselves. The individual may just have better luck because with PR, sometimes editors, if they hear "PR," will hang up the phone because of stocky PR people. One of the things at Siren, we try not to be stocky PR people. We develop relationships, so I can call an editor and say, "Hey, how's your boyfriend? How was your vacation at Las Ventanas?" You're developing a relationship and not being a stalker and understanding that editors are slammed busy. They have a million things going on, and you may be calling at a really bad time. Ninety-nine-point-nine percent of the time, you are. Don't just call an editor and say, "Did you get it? Did you like it? Are you going to feature it?" You have to have a conversation [because] you're developing a relationship.

Don't just call an editor and say, "Did you get it? Did you like it? Are you going to feature it?" You have to have a conversation [because] you're developing a relationship.

With boutiques, you say, "Who do I talk to about sales?" You have to do a lot of talk and knock. Starting locally is always the best idea because then you can go into the national magazines and say, "Look, I've already created this phenomenon." Leverage the press that you already have to get more press. That's what you do. Whenever any of our clients get an article in *Vogue*, they send that out to the top 200 newspapers nationwide. Because by getting something in *Vogue*, you can get all the newspapers. TV follows newspaper a lot

When you're getting started, you have to be your own publicist.

of the time. Suddenly people will read something they see in the *LA Times* and say, "Oh, that's a trend. We want to do a segment on that." It just generates press, begets press.

Another thing I always say you should do is try to get celebrity stylists to come into the showroom. Whenever you hear on TV or read in *Us Weekly* or *People*, so-and-so, Jessica Simpson's stylist, loves to go into Scoop to pick out clothes, you have her name. You just have to do some digging and then invite her in to take a look at what you have. And then you get a celebrity to wear it, and you can get press off of that.

It's all research. Track down the source. Google them. That's an amazing way to get into touch. If I'm trying to get to a celebrity makeup artist, like if I want to know who does Jennifer Garner's makeup, I'll go to movies that Jennifer's been in, look at the credits for the makeup artist on the film. Then call whatever film studio produced it and say, "Do you have contact info for so-and-so?" When you talk to them, say, "Hey, I have some really cool stuff I'd love to show you. Can I send you a package? I know you work with Jennifer Garner. I'd love to send the latest, greatest, not-even-in-stores-yet." Maybe she'll like it. Then you develop a relationship with whomever you're trying to target. Hopefully, Jennifer Garner will fall in love with whatever it is you've sent. Then you just have to go about getting permission to use the celebrity's name.

Once her stylist says she loves this certain scarf, for instance, you go to her publicist and say, "Her stylist says she loves this scarf. Is it OK if I use her name for an article I'm working on with *InStyle*?"

When you're getting started, you have to be your own publicist. Ultimately, you're just looking for that one editor who has a minute, is in a good mood, and needs an idea for a story. That can make you. When I first started out, I didn't know anybody. I had to introduce myself. My first three years, I went to lunches and dinners and cocktails every single night of the week. That was how I got to meet people. And you end up talking about everything but work for most of the time. It's relationship building. You can start with an editorial assistant or an assistant editor. But those people in five years are going to be the fashion director. The other thing is that if you're young, you'll find that the editors are going to be young, cool, interesting people with their own stories to tell.

Another thing that's very important is to read the magazines and know the different sections you want to get in. Pitch for a specific section of the magazine. Say, "I love what you wrote about XYZ. I have something that could work really well."

The last thing is, know your market. Know whether your stuff belongs in *Cosmo* or *Teen People* or *Vogue*. Don't pitch something that costs $5,000 to *Teen People* because they're never going to cover it. You must know your target audience.

Melissa Joy Manning on Being Discouraged

Designer Melissa Joy Manning's jewelry can be found in more than 200 stores in the United States, Canada, Australia, Saudi Arabia, and Japan. Her pieces have been featured in numerous television programs, feature films, and fashion magazines. Melissa's celebrity clients include Sheryl Crow, Cameron Diaz, Lucy Liu, Sandra Bullock, Venus Williams, Serena Williams, Jewel, and Pink.

I've made jewelry since I was in Montessori school, but it was never like I wanted to be a jewelry designer. I mean, I used to lay on the floor of my house as a kid with my friends and we used to draw fashion magazines, and I always had this idea that in one way or another I would be in one, or something I made would be. I made friendship bracelets and put material on the sides of my jeans. My mother always said I could be whatever I wanted to be, but my dad always was like, "You can't ever make a living in art, you need to fall back on something," so I never thought of being a jewelry designer. In fact, it was one of those things I never really knew ever existed.

When I left college, I was working in restaurants and high-end retail. I had no career aspirations, didn't really know what I was going to do with myself, and my mom sent me to a vocational counselor. And all the tests came out that I should be self-employed.

I'm not difficult, but I have a definite idea of how things should be done. And I'm one of those people that if someone shows me how to do something, I immediately devise my own way to do it so that I can get it done faster for me personally, which causes problems in an office environment because then other people are like, "You're working too fast," or, "I don't like your initiative." At 24, no one wants to deal with someone like that. They want you to do what you're told and punch the clock and leave and come in, and that's not a work ethic I have. So the vocational counselor asked me what I could do, and I said I could make jewelry, and they were like, well, there you go.

I had no startup money. I think I was on unemployment at the time because I had gotten fired again, which was a bonus because then I had some kind of fallback—about $300 a month—and I was 25 at the time with four roommates, so it was OK. We were living in a flat in San Francisco before the tech boom so everything around was cheap, and I was working out of someone's garage so I had no overhead.

I started the business on a consignment basis with one store in San Francisco. I realized I needed more experience, so I went back to work for a jewelry company as a sales and marketing manager and did some of the trade-show setup and mailers and other sales, and again got fired. Again it was office politics. It was 14 girls in one office, and I was brought in as a manager at 25 and traveled all over and was never in the office and just didn't foster a relationship with anyone. So I got fired again. I remember one day I was crying, "What am I ever going to do?" literally crying in front of the television. Then the show *Just Shoot Me!* came on, and this girl walks across the screen and she's wearing my necklace. I called the show, they were like, "Yeah, she got it in San Francisco when she was on vacation, she insisted on wearing it because she loved it so much, it was her good-luck piece." I was like, "All right, that's a sign." So that's when I went into it full-force and realized that this is what I'm supposed to be doing, and I'm not ever going to look back.

About a year later I did look back; things weren't going that well. I think I had done like $15,000 in sales, I was only working with a couple of stores, I was doing street fairs, and I had no money in the bank. Again, feeling sorry for myself and literally in tears, I turned on the television and the same exact rerun of *Just Shoot Me!* is on. And I was like wow, OK, a believer.

That was six years ago. I now have eight or nine employees and we're doing quite well. So I do have a dream job, but I have to say it that it hasn't always been a dream. I've gotten to an amazing point where I am lucky enough to love what I do, and I've loved every single minute of it, but it's definitely been a struggle. It's been something where I've been hard to be around; it's been my marriage of sorts for the last six years. I have created a dream career, but it's definitely not like somebody gave me a bunch of money, I showed [my jewelry] at a market, and suddenly everyone wanted my products.

It took at least two years to get past the street-fair stage. I had no startup money, so what I was doing was really just investing [any money I made] back into the business. I had devised my strategy with an aggressive trade-out policy so if a store tried my product [and] it didn't sell for them, I said I would trade it out at full value against their next order, so that they would be guaranteed that they would order again and I would continue the client relationship. But I then would take all this stock back, so I would have to liquidate it, and that's why I was doing street fairs. So I did those for the first couple years, and then broke up with a boyfriend and was like, "Eh, I'm not depending on anyone else but myself; I really need to do this." I started researching, and I had enough in the bank at that point to test-market three trade shows, so I test-marketed the gift, the craft, and the fashion shows.

For any product there's different markets for your channels of distribution. So for me, as a jeweler, I can choose to sell at a craft level—gallery or museum gift shops; gift level, at stores that sell random gifts; or the fashion market, where I am now, which is both high-end boutiques and department stores. I started doing both gift and fashion for a while, dropped gift after a year, and then went straight into fashion, and that's where we do the entirety of our business. We're in over 200 stores.

I think for a jewelry designer, especially now, it's not necessarily about being the best designer—you have to be an entrepreneur, you have to know the market, you have to be able to find a niche, and you have to be able to target your customers. I did a business program called the Renaissance Center. I don't think it's available everywhere, but they have sister organizations, and it's a business center where you have to a have a viable business idea to be accepted, and then they help you devise a business plan and kind of tell you how to do a business.

It's not necessarily about being the best designer. You have to be an entrepreneur.

So besides developing your product, I would say it's equally important to develop a business philosophy, one that will drive you, and a vision that can drive you through different stages of your development so that you have an idea of where you want to be, whether it's dollar amounts, stores you want to be in, employees, any of those kind of things because those—those are what drive me. I always set new visions and new goals every quarter, and then we issue those and move forward, so it becomes less about this grand idea of "I want to be a jewelry designer," but you can break it down into easier goals of achieving different levels within being a jewelry designer.

Take every *no* not as a no but as an inquiry to further your product to make it better.

But my main piece of advice is to never give up. I mean, I used to leave New York in tears because Barneys would never look at me— and now they're one of my best clients and have been for three years. So I would take every *no* not as a no but as an inquiry to further your product to make it better. If you're doing something truly innovative, you might not be picked up right away, but the market will come back around and you'll be recognized as such. So it might take a while, but you'll create longevity in the business, which is much better than being trend driven.

If you put your heart and soul into something and that's what you want to be, you will eventually be successful, even if it's not your original idea of what success is. It just takes a while for everything to come together.

Elizabeth Bell on How to Get Department Store Buyers to Come to Your Shows

Elizabeth Bell is an associate buyer for Contemporary Collection at Saks Fifth Avenue.

A buyer is responsible for everything that goes in and out of stores. It's not as fun as it seems—people think you go to all these fashion shows, and you do, but 80–90 percent of it is financials. It's like you're running your own business. So you have to understand math. Not hard numbers, but you kind of have to have a grasp of the big picture. You go to a fashion show and then you go to a person's showroom. You pick out what you like and what you think is going to do well. And you go back to the office and say, "I really like this. I'm going to buy 20 for New York, 10 for Boston." You pretty much pick out what you want to go to each store.

If a lot of the stuff you picked out didn't do very well, you could try to negotiate returns to the vendor, saying, "This dress was awful. It didn't do very well for us. Can you take these back and give us back our money?" Also, at a certain point, you say, "This has been in our store for 12 weeks. . . " You're responsible for figuring out the markdowns.

Especially in contemporary, you can go in and say, "This is beautiful. This is going to sell well." But in our area, we always joke that some of the stuff is just [so] different and out there that you never know what's going to sell well. It's really a gamble. Especially in contemporary. For the most part, Saks is trying to focus on things that are unique. If we go and see a red coat with a belt, we'll say, "Oh, wow, that's really pretty, but you could get that at Banana Republic." We try to get things that are going to differentiate us.

With the little guys, especially when they're building their business, I would guess that we wouldn't expect them to take things back or give us money for markdowns. At Saks, because we have so many stores, a lot of times the little vendors can't. They end up building themselves up at boutiques. Even when we have found some [little] vendors who are amazing, a lot of times they can't keep up with the volume. Their deliveries are off. It ends up not being a good thing for us. Like, if we advertise something in a catalog—we have to print the catalog so far in advance—if it ends up not being on the floor by the time the catalog drops, it's a big deal. It's really frustrating for the customer. Little vendors often have production issues. They just can't always produce everything on time. They're still figuring things out, and still getting it together. They're not as reliable as the big guys. I think the little vendors are great because they differentiate you from other specialty stores. But there's a little bit of risk involved.

Little vendors are great because they differentiate you from other specialty stores. But there's a little bit of risk involved.

In my old area [cosmetics and accessories], I would say I got about 10 calls a day from new vendors, and there was no way we could possibly meet with everyone. What we would do is have them send us their product. If it looks like something we might be interested in, we would call them in for a meeting or go to their showroom and see them.

We saw so much junk. Some of it was really off-color. One product was for hygiene in your private areas and the vendor was like, "It tastes good, too!" And we're like, "This is Saks Fifth Avenue." Some people don't get it. Now that I'm in apparel, I'm not getting as many calls from new vendors.

We definitely have to be open to see things. Because you never know who's going to be the next Vera Wang, or whatever. We definitely try to keep an open mind and see everyone. Because you don't want to miss the next big thing.

Sending your product is always a good thing. Or if you can't send product, sending pictures is good. It really helps to see it on, though, so send a picture of someone actually wearing the dress, for example. If it looks like something Saks would buy and is in our price-point range, the next step is setting up an appointment.

Generally, people include price-point information. If the price points aren't where they need to be, some vendors will say, "We can make it more expensive." But that's not the point. Anybody can mark up a product. We want it to be something that you put that much time and creativity into so that it's at $400 for a reason, not because you're making too much money on it. Generally,

We definitely have to be open to see things. Because you never know who's going to be the next Vera Wang.

vendors list wholesale price. They can't dictate retail prices; it's illegal.

What some small vendors can do is sell their stuff on consignment. If it's something that we don't necessarily have a lot of money for and are nervous about the liability, there are some consignment opportunities, especially in jewelry. So it doesn't go into our "on hand" [unsold merchandise totals], which is nice. So if we make a sale, then we make a sale and the money goes to the vendor. If it's something that people really believe in, there's a chance. From what I've seen, a lot of times the small vendors will build themselves at the small boutiques and build their business that way.

Good buyers know that it's important to see those little guys because you never know who's coming out with the next pet rock. I definitely think it's important. Sometimes they'll come and you'll say, "This is great, but you're not even set up with a factory yet. Call me back in a year. Get yourself going. And then, I love your stuff, so I'll be happy to meet you." That type of thing. The key is to keep the communication going.

The Aspiring Director

There's only one director per play, you know," says Oliver. "You figure most do it until they're 75 or 80. Unless you're senile, you can direct until you die. So there just aren't that many openings or much turnover." Fortunately (or unfortunately, depending on your vantage point), no one's going to die in the directing chapter on my watch, unless it's from being a starving artist. But as even that is within the realm of possibility, I probably shouldn't joke about it.

Oliver's been interested in the theater for 25 of his 27 years. He works out of his home. (Someone pays him to do something. It's not illegal; it's just not that interesting.) And so, blessed, he spends seven hours on the internet each day trolling for information about grants. Before going any further, I must tell you that Oliver is quite dashing. So please, when reading about Oliver, to the best of your ability imagine

John Heard, the sexy, skirt-chasing theater director who had the misfortune of being married to Bette Midler's character in *Beaches*. Only Oliver's not troubled in any of those ways, and in fact, the absolute first thing he does every morning is walk his girlfriend to the subway so that he can spend time with her before she leaves for work.

Oliver lays out a somewhat dismal financial projection: As a young director, if you work like a maniac doing overlapping plays, up to six per year—it's simply not possible to take on any more—you could earn between $18,000 and $36,000 annually if every project paid you for your work. As it happens, however, most young directors work for free. But Oliver has his heart set on directing until he's dead or senile. (As cliché as it sounds, that kind of commitment really is critical for success in the arts.) Therefore, he's determined that if he ever wants to have children, he's going to have to diversify so that his income comes from grants, a teaching gig, an acting program, books he writes, and a commercial show that runs for a while and pays residuals.

Unless you're senile, you can direct until you die. So there just aren't that many openings or much turnover.

In the meantime, Oliver sends out 1,500 letters a year—"a pretty professional package of stuff"—everything from positive reviews his plays have received to proposals for regional theaters like, "Would you consider this show for your next season?"

He's gotten four responses. The first two were inconclusive in that thanks-for-the-update way. The third was an annoying, that-person-doesn't-work-here-anymore-please-take-me-off-your-mailing-list zinger, and the fourth was a note from a former professor who said, "Thanks for keeping me in the loop all these years. Oliver, have I got a job for you." The job was a lovely but short two-month post at Brandeis University.

When I talk to Oliver, it's a Saturday afternoon in the summer, and he's on his way to a honky-tonk bar called Moonshine, where he's hosting a fundraiser BBQ for a movie he's the artistic director for. At $10 for a two-hour open bar, it's a gluttonously good deal. Oliver's in charge of grilling all the hot dogs and hamburgers—death by starvation staved off for at least another day. What's on his mind, though, is how do you find the people who know investors? And what are organizations looking for in a winning grant proposal? "These days," he says, "I'm stressed out most of the time."

> **How do you find the people who know investors? And what are organizations looking for in a winning grant proposal?**

Jesse Peretz On What's Better Than Networking

Jesse Peretz's first feature film First Love, Last Rites *(1997) is based on an Ian McEwan short story. He also directed* The Chateau *(2001) starring Paul Rudd and music videos for the Foo Fighters. Before that, he played bass with the Lemonheads.*

A lot of younger people say, "Oh I really think I want to direct movies and I just don't know what to do; it seems that everything is so expensive." But with technology now, there are opportunities for people to make their own little video films even if they don't look so great. You can start making and shooting films on digital video and editing them on the computer, and you have a lot more flexibility than when I started out shooting on Super 8 film.

I think it's possible to break down the process of filmmaking into little pieces that you conquer one at a time. Sometimes you focus on one part and sometimes you focus on another. A lot of directors out there don't really understand the way photography works, but on the other hand, you have a whole world of directors who came through music videos and commercials who are really good at the visual aspect of moviemaking but are not good at dealing with actors. You *can* be a director without understanding cinematography or lenses or anything like that, especially if you have a good producer who hooks you up with a good cinematographer, but it seems like the really great directors understand both the acting side of moviemaking and also the photographic visual side. Martin Scorsese comes to mind—Scorsese is obviously a photographic master and a dramatic master.

In my mid twenties, I realized I was one of those people who was much more comfortable with the visual side of filmmaking. I was really nervous about actually having the language or the ability to talk with actors about acting. I was in the very early phases of working on my first feature, and I happened to be on tour with this band in Australia. I met a friend of my sister's who had just spent all this time with the director Jane Campion. She had just finished making *Angel at my Table*, but I had been totally obsessed with her movie *Sweetie*. I got her number from this friend, and I wrote a letter telling her that I was a huge fan and maybe this is totally inappropriate but would you be willing to have a cup of coffee. She was just going off to New Zealand to go do scouting for *The Piano*, but I went and did errands with her and we had a cup of coffee. I was telling her how much I loved *Sweetie* and how I loved all the weird compositions, and she got really rough with me about her own work. She said, "I just shot it that way because I was scared of actors." She asked me, "Do you feel comfortable with actors?" And I said no. She encouraged me to conquer that fear by coming home and finding actor friends and playwright friends of mine and coming together to direct some plays.

So in the years following I directed a few plays, which is something I had never tried to do before. Basically we self-financed the whole thing. You can get actors so easily. We put just ads in *Backstage* magazine for open calls for something that had basically no name, nothing, and we had 500 actors waiting at the exact time at our open-call meeting. (Granted, a lot of them totally sucked.) We did things on the cheap, and we got favors from everybody, and then we charged $5 or something like that. It was the scariest thing, but if you think about it, the directors who do movies that have incredible performances—like Mike Lee or Ken Loach—they are people who come out of the theater.

People are only psyched to invest money in new talent when they see something that's exciting and different rather than being like someone's who's managed to rip off something mediocre that they've seen in the past.

Also go and buy a 35mm camera and do photography. Understand the way light works on film and how the lenses change how the images look. Play around with the apertures so you understand compositional basics. Experiment. You should be taking pictures all the time. A lot of directors also draw comics and draw little storyboards, and that's another way to think about storytelling visually.

I think a lot of people think there is some magic in networking, and being invited to parties with cool actors and producers. I think that can be a helpful element at some point, but I think people put a lot of weight on the "If I only knew blah blah blah" and I just don't think that really ends up being a ticket to anything, especially if you don't have anything to show those people. One of the most useful things to convince someone to let you direct is being able to say, "Here is the short movie that I made with my friends and here are photographs I've taken that show that I have a really clear vision." It really comes down to owning material that is yours combined with being able to demonstrate that you have a vision of how to execute it. And once you have that, there is something that can be gotten out of networking. Ultimately, people are only psyched to invest money in new talent when they see something that's exciting and different rather than being like someone's who's managed to rip off something mediocre that they've seen in the past.

The other key thing for people who want to make movies—and weirdly enough, I didn't exactly do this—is to write a really good script. The one thing the world is always looking for is a really good script. It's really hard to write one and there are shitloads of people trying to write really good scripts and most of them suck. So if you do have a really good script and you really want to direct it, you suddenly have a certain power. There are places where you can submit scripts, like the Sundance Workshop, and you don't need the entrée of a powerful person to get stuff read. They're psyched to discover people. And if you can demonstrate that you have a vision, then you get a shot at meeting people who will put a stamp of approval on it and will open other doors for you to get it out there.

It took me about five years to get my first feature made. It took forever. There's nothing easy about getting your first movie made. In the early stages, I was working on a screenplay with a friend who was more of a writer than me, and it took us a very long time to learn that we needed to actually get the rights to the story, which was an Ian McEwan short story. Eventually I met somebody and I was talking to her about the script, and she recommended that I give it to these two producers, Scott Macaulay and Robin O'Hara, because she said Scott Macaulay loved Ian McEwan and they had produced a couple low-budget things together.

I sent them the script, and they later told me they were totally prepared to hate it because they loved the story so much. They ended up liking it though, and we had a meeting where I showed them a couple of short films—pretty bad short films that I made—and somehow we got along well and they thought I had a good idea of what I wanted this movie to be. They helped me get the rights, but that still took a year because they weren't big producers and I was a first-time director. Eventually we got the rights contingent on Ian liking the script. He became a real advocate for us, but even with him supporting it and having producers it took us another two years to pull together the $450,000 that we needed. If it had been a more commercial script it might have been an easier thing to set up, but eventually the producers got the money by making a deal with this super-rich businessman who wanted to make a movie—they would produce his movie if he would finance half of mine. Then we basically formed a little corporation and scraped together the remaining $175,000 from you know, $10,000 from my grandmother, $10,000 from my parents. I did a bunch of commercials and I put $20,000 into it, my friend Donald Lowe who's an actor put $20,000 into it. I don't think anyone's made all of their money back yet. The thing is we also can only do that once because people aren't going to invest again unless they get their money back. So even with lots of good resources working for you, its still super hard.

Jenny Gersten on How to Become Known

When I talked to Jenny Gersten, she was an associate producer of the Williamstown Theater Festival, the crème de la crème of summer theater in western Massachusetts where Gwyneth Paltrow cut her teeth. During Jenny's nine years with WTF, *the festival garnered the Tony Award for best regional theater and was responsible for six productions transferring to Broadway. Since then, Jenny has moved on to become the artistic director for a theater company in New York called Naked Angels, which is devoted to the development and production of new works.*

Williamstown isn't a theater festival in the traditional sense, like the Fringe Festival of Edinburgh. Williamstown Theater is more of a regional theater in the sense that we start with a play or a director and produce our own shows.

At Williamstown, we have a bunch of different programs for young directors—mostly directors in graduate school, and some undergraduates, and some career directors. We have an internship program, we have a director assistantship program, and we have two directing fellowships. We sort of move young directors through the pipeline. You apply on our website, and then we do an interview. Sometimes we go see a show, but oftentimes it's a videotape.

I think we try to take a motley crew of directors because it's nice to have that in the program, to have a bunch of different influences. But overall, it's people who are articulate and people who seem to have a specific kind of vision and are very clear about the kinds of shows they want to direct or how they want to direct theater or what they like about theater. If they

If they can articulate [their vision] clearly, that's something we respond to. It helps if they're not crazy. We try to avoid crazy people.

can articulate that clearly, that's something we respond to. It helps if they're not crazy. We try to avoid crazy people. But it really runs the gamut.

The internships and the assistantships are both nine-week programs. They come up and direct the nonprofessional actors at the festival, and they do late-night projects with them as well as assist directors on our professional shows. So they assist one show and then direct a late-night project.

The interns and assistants pay for housing, which is $500, and they themselves don't get paid. But it's an automatic opportunity to work with professional directors and connect for a while, and they're also meeting the future generation of their collaborators—the young actors and directors they'll work with later. I think Williamstown on a resume does raise eyebrows. It is a noticeable credit.

My friend, who is 26, went through all those levels and is now assisting on a Broadway show at Lincoln Center, and that's what he's been doing—trying to assist professional directors to pay the bills and also direct his own shows. His crisis is, "How do I transition from basically an unknown director to a known director? How do I get people to call me to direct things?"

He got one piece of advice from an agent who said, "Go to every opening-night party you can. Get out there. Be seen. Show you're an active part of the theater community."

> **Go to every opening-night party you can. Get out there. Be seen. Show you're an active part of the theater community.**

There's a million different ways to go about it. Sometimes I say start your own theater company, do your own shows. Once you do your own shows and create a buzz, your name will start surfacing more and more. Unfortunately it costs money to do that, and it's hard to find that money. Another way to do [it] is just meet playwrights. Find writers and get their scripts, and then go to a theater with a script in hand as opposed to just, "I'm a director and I want to direct a play." Have a young writer the theater might really be interested in.

If the director is aligned with the writer and the theater then invites the writer to do that play, hopefully the writer will say, "Well, you have to have this director direct my play; he's my collaborator."

At least with a writer, you can send a play. But directors, when you send pictures and reviews, it's very difficult to translate [those] into, "How is this person going to create a play and lead a cast and work with our theater company?"

You can go to Edinburgh Fringe Festival, and basically for that you have to come up with a show people will want to see and then present it in a really fun way so the festival takes it, which isn't that different from sending it to a film festival.

As an associate producer, I do a bunch of different things. I oversee the hiring of the nonprofessional acting company. I go to auditions and I help pick those actors. I raise money and I do marketing, I do the literary stuff, I read new plays. I read a couple hundred plays a year. I'm lucky because I also get to pick the plays that we do for our reading series, although our producer picks the professional shows. So if I really like a new play, I'll do a reading of it. We usually do six to eight readings a year.

We have a pretty strict policy of agent submissions only, which is pretty common for most American theaters. It's very controversial because there are a lot of writers out there who

There are a lot of writers out there who don't have agents. The problem is, there are a lot of writers who don't have agents because they're not very good.

don't have agents. The problem is, there are a lot of writers who don't have agents because they're not very good. But on the other hand, how do you break through? To keep things fresh, I try to read a couple plays per year that aren't through an agent. I'll break down if someone calls me. I'm a total softie.

At Williamstown, there's a non-equity company, and there's an apprentice company. The 70 apprentices take classes and seminars and then have rotating production assignments. They work really, really hard. They're kind of the backbone of the festival, and they pay a lot of money to be there and be our labor force. But they also get to audition for small roles in the professional productions we do.

The non-equity company is a smaller company—usually 20 or fewer grad school–level actors. They audition for bigger [yet still] small roles in the professional shows and also do late-night projects with the assistant directors, not the interns.

I have great parents who both work in nonprofit arts, and I always knew I wanted to work in theater. I got a job out of college working at a theater for inner-city kids, and I met a stage manager there who a few years later got the artistic director job here, and he hired me. I've been here for nine years.

There was a guy once who came to Williamstown as a directing assistant and did really interesting work, so we had him back the next year as a fellow and he did really interesting work. So then we said, "Well, maybe you should direct the outdoor theater." And then we were like, "Wow, you were really good at that; will you come back and do it again?" So he did it again, and he got a show on the little stage, and then he got a main stage show, and then he got an agent, and a directing career. He got all kinds of fellowships and grants. And that's one in a hundred, but it's a good story.

Ken Chu on How to Write a Winning Grant Proposal

Program director Ken Chu oversees and implements the grant-making selection process for Visual Arts and Emerging Fields for the Creative Capital Foundation, a New York City–based nonprofit organization created to support individual emerging artists. For artists, Creative Capital is the Holy Grail of funding.

If you look at most professions, once you come out of college you kind of fall into an internship phase, and that's where you pick up the kind of practical skills that you need to survive in your field. And with film and performance arts, you work on a collaborative project together. You work on a film project which requires a crew, and you learn about the different roles people play in there and all the kinds of skills and talent it takes to put together a project. Whereas in visual arts, that doesn't exist—you come out of college and you're basically on your own. What visual artists need to know is to look at the arts ecosystem and [to realize] that there are galleries that specialize in entry-level artists, that provide opportunities for you to show. Then you look at organizations that are looking at emerging artists, and you kind of work your way up the scales to museums and the arts institutions . . . using the organizations as markers for your career as you progress. It's kind of the support system for artists.

Creative Capital is one of the major organizations that looks at emerging artists. It's a pretty involved process that we do. Basically, we provide financial support for an artist's project, and then we also provide professional development training to the artist. Because of that, our whole submission process is kind of designed as a skills-honing workshop for the artist.

What visual artists need to know is that they need to look at the arts ecosystem.

So what we ask the artists to do is submit a letter of inquiry, and unlike other application processes, in this first phase we don't ask them to submit work samples. Everything is evaluated on the way they are able to articulate their projects and their art form.

Questions that we pose on the inquiry form are basically information that you would need to put on a letter of inquiry or a letter of intent if you're approaching people who aren't in the field. Like if you're a filmmaker, you need certain equipment or supplies or in-kind contributions—you know, corporate sponsorships, etc.; you need to speak the language. Not even plain English, more like dollar signs.

The way we see it, the arts culture is a gift culture. As the artist, you create a piece and then you kind of give it to the community or the society you live in, something that you've shared. Whereas the culture we predominantly live in, the society is more of a commerce-driven culture. So we're looking to train our artists to kind of speak that language—to put a dollar sign to how much your time is worth. If you speak to people outside of the arts, that's basically all they want to know: how much are you asking for, how much you want to get paid for. It's important for the artists to learn how to quantify that. If you're an emerging artist and you're slapping on several hundred thousand dollars for your piece, of course that's absurd. You have to be in touch with your peer group and find out what your peers are charging for their pieces. That's basically what we're looking for in that very initial stage of the application process.

We ask [applicants] to fill out a written form, and these are the same questions that you can actually apply in drafting a press release. The questions are basically: Tell us about your project and tell us where this idea comes from; place it into a context for us. And then look at who is your audience; where are the places you want to take your pieces? We want to get an idea of whether they understand the arts ecosystem.

For a typical round of applications we get about 3,000 inquiries. We look at two disciplines per year, so I usually get the majority of them. The best inquiries are the ones who are really concise and basically that's it. You have to think about having yourself in my seat. If you are looking at 1,200 proposals, which one do you think is going to stick out for you? And the ones that are most concise and most clearly articulated are the ones that are going to pop up. It's got to be memorable.

Doing the homework is really important. We post everything on our website — our schedule is on the website, the process is explained, our focus is explained there, so if they haven't made the effort to look up what we do and who we are, then I really don't have an interest in their solicitation. I know that's one of the main complaints of gallerists because they have to process thousands of slides a week of artists who kind of send in slides cold. It's really frustrating because the artists really haven't done any research as to what type of work the gallery is interested in, what type of work they're supporting, who their buyers are, who their audiences are. The more research you do on the front end of developing a project, the greater impact it will have at the end. By finding out which critics would need to see your work or somebody who has written about your work, then those are the people you need to think about in the beginning of your project. You have to start formulating in your mind a press release of how you're going to phrase things and whom you're targeting this work for.

Before they send off their application, the artist should get somebody who is not familiar with their work [and] is not in their field to take a look at it. And if they can visualize the piece enough to understand what is it [you're] doing, then I think that's when you're ready to send it.

Start formulating in your mind a press release of how you're going to phrase things and whom you're targeting this work for.

They should be resourceful in writing about the work, to feel free to quote critics or other sources that have written about them.

Basically with a great proposal, you get a sense of sincerity. It comes out in the writing. There isn't really any specific way to write it. As long as I can get a sense of who you are as a human being, that's what stays with me through the whole process, and that's what I take with me as I basically walk these proposals through the whole process. After the letter of inquiry, the number of proposals we're considering gets cut down to about 300 artists that we invite to come back with a formal application, and that's when we ask for the work samples. At that point, there's a greater chance for them to make it to the final round, so it would be worth [it] for them to invest money for sending the work samples. Otherwise, it's really expensive for all these artists to be sending us slides or videotapes, and it's impractical for us to try and evaluate them, too.

At the next stage, we work with a group of arts professionals around the country to help us review and identify a group of 125 artists that we move on to the panel level. At the panel level, we bring in our esteemed colleagues from around the country—we have affiliations with different institutions as well as artists—and select 20 recommendations for our board. So in the end, it's like 2 percent of the application pool.

When we look at the work samples, we're looking at the way the ideas are rendered—how it's realized and how the personality comes through your art form. Art is very much about the personality. Otherwise, what is going to distinguish yourself from your peer, your neighbor, or even your mentor who has inspired you? We're not looking for everybody to come in sounding like David Mamet. Yes, maybe he has

We're not looking for everybody to come in sounding like David Mamet.

inspired you or informed your work, but we want to hear your interpretation of it or how this has influenced your work. We're looking at individuals. And we're really looking at the personality because we are committed to our artists on a long-term basis, unlike other grants. We work with the artists anywhere between three to five years because we recognize the whole cycle, what it takes to create a piece, and to premiere it, and to stay with the projects afterwards instead of just going on to the next one. Because once the project is premiered, that's when the life of the project starts, and that's when most artists are kind of burned-out and ready to move on.

The initial grants that we give are anywhere from $5,000 to $20,000. And we have supplementary money that is put aside for each artist that they can access at any time of their partnership with us for more specific needs like materials. The grants are open grants—you can use it for whatever your needs are. There are no strings attached to the money, so you can use it to fly to Europe if you want, but most artists don't. They don't abuse the money at all. They are actually very diligent as to how each penny is spent for the work.

We also introduce the artists to people with funding expertise, people to help them with time management and money management, so we kind of bring on these consultants. And we bring on a strategic planner to help them kind of map out their careers, their lives. It's really a needed aspect of our field. And giving them all that, and then for them to be able to afford some of the follow-up stuff, that's what the specific money is for. We kind of have to look at setting up the administrative component of their career and not just focusing on the creation of the art. So they can hire a part-time administrator to come in and do the paperwork or to help them write a proposal, that kind of stuff. We have money set aside, if their work is accepted at a festival, so they can request travel money. Or if they are accepted at a residency, most residencies don't provide any type of stipend, and then they can request some money for that. When we start talking about the consultants and stuff, it's all new to them, so we provide money to hire PR/marketing consultants too.

One of the things we're in the process of developing right now is a system for artists to pay to attend the Institute, if they haven't been chosen. We've been around since 1999, and we found our grantees were responding more to the professional development component of our grant actually, more than the money. You know the money's wonderful; they all love it, but having this type of support has been life-changing to a lot of these artists.

Just last year, state legislators in Arizona were going to cut the whole arts budget down to zero. The state arts council decided on the day they were making the [budget-cut proposals] to have a picnic on the front lawn of the state capitol building. All the artists, their families, their

Art is not just the plaything of the privileged.

friends, just kind of planted themselves there and had a day-long picnic, and that saved the arts budget for that day. And one of the things we're really interested in [is] helping our artists participate as full citizens of this country. A lot of us have jobs, unfortunately not in the arts, but we are able to sustain our practice, and we pay taxes from our jobs. Art is not just the plaything of the privileged.

The Aspiring Gamer

Jeff, 29, is a good example of somebody who didn't know what a good thing he had when he had it. Five years ago, he was working for a catalog that featured computer parts for Macintoshes. (Just to be clear, this isn't the good part. It would be a little tragic actually if it were.) But after getting laid off from that job, he interviewed for and was offered a position at a venture-capital newsletter. "I was about to start, but I wanted to see if I could get something cooler," Jeff says. "So I kept on calling this one place I had interviewed with, Katrillion, who had never gotten back to me. I decided that they would have to tell me something; I just wanted that much, at least."

Turns out that the folks at Katrillion had really liked Jeff but "had just forgotten to call me back all these months." In the dating world, this would be considered inauspicious.

Jeff is a good example of somebody who didn't know what a good thing he had when he had it.

Nonetheless, Jeff started his job as a copy editor at Katrillion for $35,000 a year.

Katrillion was a website for teenagers. "I'm not really sure what quantity 'katrillion' denotes," Jeff says. They had a lot of jokes around the office about how *katrillion* represented the number of shares they were each going to get at the IPO, back when IPO jokes were funny.

At 24, Jeff was the resident old guy. As for every other employee there, this was literally their first job out of college. After a week or two, Jeff had some extra time on his hands, so the managing editor asked him if he wanted to start reviewing videogames. (She then called up the freelancer who'd been writing reviews and said that with Jeff, the resident videogame expert, onboard, the freelancer's services wouldn't be needed anymore.)

Jeff hadn't played a videogame in seven years.

"So I immediately started studying Pokémon, which is a weird thing to study," he says. "I called Nintendo, and Nintendo put me on the mailing list, so whenever a new game came out, they would send it to me." Jeff would write a 150-word review for the website, touching on little more than if it was good or not—and why. "I think the way [some] professional videogame reviewers work is they play the whole game until it's done," he says. "Just like, if you review a movie, you see it. And with a CD, you listen to it once or twice. But a game can be like 45 hours long, to get to one of eight multiple endings. So there really was no way I could play the whole game. Different reviewers have different cut-off points at which they say, 'OK, I've played enough to say if it's good or not.' Mine was an hour or so. Then we would move on to the next game."

Jeff did that for about nine months, during which time he was promoted to senior editor and soon found himself evaluating videogames full-time. But then he did something "really stupid" that got him fired from the company.

They had a lot of jokes around the office about how *katrillion* represented the number of shares they were each going to get at the IPO, back when IPO jokes were funny.

"Did you ever see the first 10 minutes of *Jerry Maguire* where he gets all motivated and writes this inspirational memo to everyone?" Jeff asks. "That's what I did, more or less." He explains that a new editor in chief was starting at Katrillion — someone who was dramatically changing the direction of the website. "He wanted to be the *Washington Post* of teen websites." To that end, every article needed to be an exclusive, with new information about "Britney Spears or hair dye." Jeff says his mistake was not in sending the memo to the president of the company, but in not letting the president know that it was also sent company-wide. Jeff sent the email, entitled "Necrosis," a medical term for the death of tissues through disease, at the end of what must have been a largely unproductive day. "It was 3:30 in the morning and I was still trying to get my daily stuff done, which is supposed to be done at 5 p.m.," he says.

Jeff's boss waited a few days before firing him. "Apparently, she had been hoping I would have just apologized for sending the memo out. I didn't want to do that. It was kind of a weird place to make a stand, but I was 25 at the time and feeling more adventurous careerwise than I am now."

That was May, and Jeff spent the better part of the summer reading, watching movies, and applying for jobs. He couldn't find anything. At the end of the summer he "sucked it up" and wrote an apology letter saying that he'd like to make it up to Katrillion and come back to work. Jeff's hiatus was heretofore known as his summer sabbatical. A month later on September 11, 2001, one of the Katrillion staffers was outside smoking a cigarette and saw one of the hijacked planes overhead. "We shifted our coverage for a week or so—no more stupid Britney Spears, Christina Aguillera stuff. We just wrote about the war and how it affected kids. And it felt really good to actually do something and have it mean something, instead of just sitting futilely by the television."

Four months later, Jeff's boss called the full staff in for a meeting and explained that Katrillion was closing down. "The next two hours turned into a free-for-all where everyone was grabbing anything of value and putting it in their car. I got a *Simpsons* poster. Me and six other guys who played games divided up the videogame library. I knew the unopened games I could return to Wal-Mart for food money, so I just took those." The whole sequence reminds me of the "record store challenge" episode you see in sitcoms like *Roseanne* or *Happy Days*, when you get 10 minutes to make off with as many LPs as you can manage. "One guy waited until our boss opened the 'prize library' and he walked out with a stack of Xboxes, which he sold on eBay. Most of the other office equipment was just sold for cents on the dollar or just thrown away," he says, "so I ultimately didn't feel bad that we all ransacked the place."

It wasn't until the next day that Jeff realized he would be competing against the 20 other members of the Katrillion editorial staff, who all had had roughly the same job responsibilities, for the same two relevant job openings available at the time. "I found one videogame reviewer position in the nine months I was looking," he says, "but it was somewhere in Nebraska, and I think it was only an internship." On his resume, he started "broadening" the description of his work experience—from "game reviewer" to "technology reporter for a website for teenagers" to, finally, "technology and news reporter," which in all kindness, is a complete stretch. "Looking for a job is difficult enough when you have qualifications. My only ones were being able to tell you how much better this year's Madden NFL game was from last year's," he emailed me.

Jeff eventually landed a freelance job copyediting for publications put out by hospitals and drug companies. "I copyedited things that I didn't think need copyediting for Pfizer. Plates and napkins. They had this 12-step approval process all printed material—including napkins—had to go through."

Jeff now works for a healthcare magazine read by people "in the clinical trial world." He makes $34,000, which is, he admits somewhat ruefully, "one [thousand] less than what I started at [working for] Katrillion."

"The best part about working at Katrillion—as great as the people were—wasn't Katrillion itself; it was being able to tell someone at a party, 'Yeah, I review videogames for a living.' That kind of determined the whole course of the rest of the conversation, especially if it was like a young guy," says Jeff. "He would just start telling me what he would do to get my job, who he would kill."

Chris Kaye on Why Now Is a Good Time to Establish a Niche

Having worked at websites like CitySearch and AOL's *Digital City, Chris Kaye "brushed the detritus from his ironic shirt" and was able to take his interest in technology and "claw his way into writing for magazines." He is also editor-at-large for* Decibel *magazine.*

I got laid off from a dotcom in 2001, so I started freelancing pretty much hardcore. I made a list of targets of where I wanted to write, based mostly on the magazines that I liked. The main one was *Esquire*. I started writing complete pitches and basically started pestering this one editor at *Esquire* who [had] gone to my school and I sort of knew. I sent him an email saying, "I don't know if you remember me, blah blah blah," and sent him a piece. He was like, "This is good, but it's really kind of not what we're looking for." I continued to send him stuff, and we kind of talked more about what I was interested in. Each time, he rejected me. Then maybe about six months later, he called me and was like, "You're into videogames, aren't you?" And I was like, "Yeah." And he said, "Well, I need to fill some space." So as I started working for him—and these were un-bylined pieces, just small little items, and I started doing a couple every month. But from there as I did more that sort of expanded to doing, like, personal technology and gear-type stuff for them. So I started getting larger pieces, like reviewing cell phones. After the *Esquire* stuff came out, with bylines, I started getting called by other people, like *Stuff*.

Someone recommended me to do a DVD column for a free in-store magazine for this small publisher in Pennsylvania that puts together these sorts of package magazines for music-store chains. I started doing that, and I went from doing the first column, which was like three short reviews of maybe 100 words each, to where it is now, which is two pages a month.

It was accidental how I got into reviewing videogames because it wasn't my intention. I always liked videogames, but I'm not what you call a hard-core gamer. But now I'm playing a couple hours every night. I initially attempted to do a lot of that during the day, but I found that, being a worka-holic, that kind of [blew] any kind of traditional kind of workday in terms of produc-tivity, to sort of sit in front of the Xbox for two hours in the middle of the day. It just didn't feel like I was getting anything done. I make an effort to really put in a day's work in terms of writing and pitching and doing research.

The videogame industry, in a lot of ways, is sort of this

The videogame industry, in a lot of ways, is sort of this black sheep of the entire entertainment industry.

black sheep of the entire entertainment industry. It's such a young industry—there is no Pauline Kael of videogame journalism yet. There's no one who's really sort of made the form— you know what goes into a movie review, right? But that hasn't sort of crystallized; sort of the art of covering this industry tends to get either very wonky on the technical side or very fannish and kind of obsessive about details that probably don't matter to a lot of people. Or completely glossy and kind of given the short look in magazines, where there's maybe 50 to 100 words on a game at the bottom third of the page. It really hasn't hit the point where it's important to have videogame coverage in a mainstream way, but hopefully as the generation that grew up with games kind of gets on in years, you'll see more of a component in general-interest magazines.

There's plenty of sites, like IGN.com, that have amateur reviewers. They're fairly comprehensive sites about games and gaming, so they really attempt to cover every release. IGN is probably one of the premiere gaming sites on the web in terms of editorial content. And there are tons of gaming magazines, that I would think if you had [an] extensive library of clips—even if they were from online—and you were looked at as really knowing what you're talking about, then your chances are pretty good. I do know people in gaming and that's how they got in, [by] contributing reviews. They were big gamers and

I do try to do other stuff to sort of make sure I don't end up in that kind of nerd ghetto.

were well-known in the online community, often because they had their own websites.

I would say the worst thing in the world for me would be if 20 years from now I'm still doing exactly what I'm doing. Because obviously, you know, I want to grow. So while the videogame thing is such a great bread and butter [gig], I do try to do other stuff to sort of make sure I don't end up in that kind of nerd ghetto. I think that's sort of what everybody wants. I don't think anybody wants to be caged in.

Ed Byrne on What Videogame Companies Are Looking For and How to Get Your Foot in Their Door

Ed Byrne is a lead designer at Zipper Interactive in Washington State. He has also worked as a designer for Amaze Entertainment and designed Harry Potter and the Prisoner of Azkaban and Ubisoft's Splinter Cell. If you have questions about "level design" and Harry Potter, Ed Byrne's your man. If you have no idea what level design is, Ed's still the man to break it down for you. He's the author of Game Level Design *and knows a tremendous amount about what it takes to make it in the gaming world.*

I know Jeff, and he was reviewing games and understands how they work. He may not understand the industry, but he understands what's fun and what isn't, and what people enjoy and what they don't. So game design is probably a good segue [for] someone who plays a lot of games. That, or being a tester.

A game designer is someone who is coming up with the ideas for the games but also creates the rules, essentially—

Part of design is knowing—referring to other games, knowing what's been done, what's been successful, what hasn't.

creates the systems and how things are meant to work and is able to tell the programmers and the artists kind of how things should look, or how different aspects of the game should be controlled. So it's a little bit like being a director on a movie. Part of what makes a good designer is knowledge of games. You can go to a special design school, you can read a bunch of books about design, but ultimately, if you're playing a lot of different types of games, it's definitely a great way to get started because part of design is knowing—referring to other games, knowing what's been done, what's been successful, what hasn't. What's interesting about game design is you're not actually *making* anything. You're not modeling, you're not doing art, you're not programming. So a lot of it is conceptual stuff; it's your knowledge of your industry and what's fun.

Videogame design is generally like designing anything else: You try to create a product that somebody's going to use, and that whoever's using it can start using it without reading a big instruction manual. The lead designer is the person who sits there and writes this big document about how it all needs to be done and look. A game writer is more akin to a scriptwriter who writes narrative or character dialogue. The level designer takes the direction of the design and actually creates a game out of it. They create the actual environments—the spaces the player will be running around in—and based on the kind of ideas and direction of the game designer, they actually go in and put the puzzles into the game levels. They'll set up the lever that you have to pull that opens the door in the next room, that sort of thing. Level designer tends to be a fairly common entry-level position now because so many kids are buying games that include software that allows them to make their own maps, that we find that we can actually hire people who have no game experience but actually have the skills already, having done that kind of stuff for fun.

A lot of times when you buy a game now, the people who made the game will actually include the tools that they used to make it. And we call those *mods*, short for *modifications*. And that's why the testing position is no longer the common position to get in on, because more and more people just have the skills that we need. But they don't have the experience—that's why they tend to come in at a low pay scale. They know how to technically operate these programs; they know the process of creating an image and bringing it into a game and putting it on a wall. What they don't know is how the industry works. They haven't worked with other people before. They don't have the experience of working within a team, of working with a client.

Until recently, there were no colleges for gaming, there were no accredited courses that were teaching you how to be a game designer or a game programmer. Now you've got any number of colleges with professional courses. For example, you've got DigiPen school in Seattle, which is basically a game-programming and design school set up by Nintendo that churns out every year a graduating class of people who have amazing skills.

A lot of the time, when you're asking about the industry, you're going to hear to get a job as a tester. Generally, testers are the people who play the game as it's being made. What they're doing is checking for bugs, which are problems in the games—like if the player just dies suddenly or a puzzle isn't solvable or the player gets into an area they shouldn't be.

Testing departments are usually huge, and they usually hire testers in to play the game night and day. Getting a job as a tester is basically about having played as many games as possible. It's an ideal position for the kind of kids who have been basically playing videogames since they were born and basically play every kind of game. It also requires an amount of dedication and perseverance. You're not playing the game; you're actually playing [as] the worst player you can imagine. You're trying to bump into walls and see which walls you can walk through, jumping off cliffs over and over again to make sure the player dies properly. But there are also other aspects. Every time you find a problem, you have to write it up—generally in a fairly complex form, give it a number, take a screen shot, and write a description of it. So good writing skills are a definite plus when you're a tester. The ability to summarize what happened in a level so that someone can fix it properly. You don't want to be going in and having a bunch of typos or not being able to explain things succinctly.

Other than that, you just have to love games and want to be a part of making them. Even if you're not creating content, you have a pretty big responsibility in making sure the game that goes out the door is good. So it's something you have to want to do. A lot of people get into the game industry as testers thinking, this is great, they get to play games all day. But they're not really playing the game for fun—they're trying to break the game, which is incredibly taxing.

Because it's an entry-level position, you don't really need any qualifications besides having played games or enjoying playing them. It tends to be the first starting position that people get into [in the professional gaming world]. The tester position is the lowest paid though. A lot of testers are kept on as contractors, so if you're a tester at a studio in LA, you might be making $30,000, but you may not be getting full benefits. Night-shift testers tend to get paid a little bit more. But it is *such* a difficult job, and the glamour is definitely not there. A lot of people go in as game testers and kind of leave after a year, realizing that they're basically working their asses off for very little money. I do have friends whose careers got started after maybe a year or two of being a tester. But the ratio of people who are testers to people who go to pursue other professional careers in the industry, like programmers or artists, is pretty low; I would say maybe 1 out of 100 testers actually gets moved up to a higher-level position.

Enid Burns on Modders

Enid has covered technology, music, film, and fashion for more than five years. Her work has appeared in more than two dozen magazines and websites, including CNN.com, FHM, Time Out New York, Nylon, ym, PC Gamer, *and* Computer Game Entertainment. *She and her husband often host* LAN *parties at their apartment, where they hook up a lot of computers together so that guests can play games en masse. Though I am still waiting to be invited to one.*

If Jeff is just looking to stay in videogames and doesn't necessarily need to stay with writing, there are a lot of possibilities. If he knows any programming, then he could probably try to get a job in various coding positions or possibly design, depending on how much experience he has with that. There are several universities, like Rensselaer in New York, that that are starting to catch on that videogame design and development are viable majors for students. I mean, the segment is growing for videogames and the technology's advancing, so there is definitely room for it.

A *modder* is someone who takes the tools in a game that allow you to make your own levels and your own environments to give the game a new playability.

I know somebody who started out as a game tester and is now a publicist at Electronic Arts. He had game experience and had gotten in with enough companies; he was able to vie for a larger position. But you could also go into product management. Product management is really like the manager of a game, so it's almost a marketing position. Maybe not entirely marketing, but you are in charge of the face of the game, so you have to work with the developers and the coders and designers. But you also work with the marketing team and PR people to coordinate how the game is going to come across.

Another interesting career path for someone who really has a lot of drive and ambition is to work on mods of games. A *modder* is someone who takes the tools in a game that allow you to make your own levels and your own environments in an existing game to give it a new playability. There have been a few examples of people who have taken a game like Battlefield 1942 and put together a mod for the game that has then caught the eye of the developer. In one case, there was a mod that was so well put-together and popular that the publisher actually bought the company of the people that put together the mod. And those people are now working on another version of Battlefield.

It used to be you made a few levels and you put something out there and you call it a mod, but now a mod keeps the same essence of the game but really changes the look of it. You'll have totally different scenery. It depends on how different they're making the game and how much they're putting into it. Someone has to be very motivated to work on something like this. There are some mods that kind of don't go anywhere, and then there are others that will take off. So it's really become an independent kind of culture.

There's a newsletter called GameDAILY.com, and probably if you're looking to get into the game industry, it's a newsletter that you should definitely consider subscribing to. They compile all the announcements of releases and any kind of breaking news, but they also have a classifieds section within the newsletter. There's also E³, the Electronic Entertainment Expo, which can be a good networking experience, and also the Game Developers Conference, which is a little bit more low-key. And that conference really caters to developers networking together, so there's probably more opportunity for someone who maybe has a demo of a game that they can show for a portfolio, for example, and there's probably more opportunity there.

The Aspiring Political Operative

Eric is and always has been passionate about public service. So right after college he and his best friend moved to Washington DC. "We got some really crappy furniture and splurged on a SEGA Saturn. At least twice a week, we ordered in one of those special pizza deals where you buy one and get one free." Do go on. "We'd each sit there with our own pizza, playing videogames, getting really fat and disgusting and horrible, and not even thinking about getting a job."

In truth, Eric is one of those idealist types, with a sense of personal responsibility to do good. Unprompted, he speaks of his political heroes, which is only slightly more unusual than the fact that he has them in the first place. I ask Eric about Eric, and he tells me about FDR's ability to lift people out of poverty through the creation of Social Security: "Government at its best really has an incredible ability to do good for a lot of people. And I wanted to help make that happen." While in DC, he spent his Saturdays tutoring an elementary-school kid in the inner city.

I don't know what kind of packaging a guy ("29, Gemini") with progress on the brain usually comes in, but when I meet Eric he's wearing a brown leather jacket with the collar turned up and smoking a cigarette. He had just moved from DC to be the New York press secretary for Howard Dean's 2004 presidential campaign. And he was no longer fat.

Eric is one of those idealist types, with a sense of personal responsibility to do good. Unprompted, he speaks of his political heroes, which is only slightly more unusual than the fact that he has them in the first place.

Eric's from suburban Philadelphia, and his parents divorced when he was 12. "I'm not sure what kind of impact that had on me. I think more than anything, kind of assuming a sense of responsibility at an age younger than a lot of guys would, just feeling that I had to take care of my mom and my sister." Eric credits his mom, a teacher, as the source of his sense of social responsibility. "Dad went through like 8 million jobs."

As Eric talks about his father's workflow cycle—from keyed-up to tapered-off interest in ventures ranging from matchmaking to selling photography packages to people planning weddings and bar mitzvahs—I think about how little long-term stability there is working in election campaigns. And that his chosen career path is, in a weird way, an amalgamation of those of his two parents. "[At one point] my dad signed on with this kind of pyramid scheme, manufacturing and selling water filters, forerunners to Brita water filters. And they'd have these marketing meetings, and my dad's all worked up—you know, 'Your body's made up of 80 percent water,' and 'Look at all the stuff that's in water. . .' Funny thing is, it was probably the right trend, he just signed on with the wrong people. Anyway, he did that for a little bit and then decided it wasn't for him."

"So I think probably seeing that, I mean, my dad after the divorce went through his midlife-crisis thing, so he was in the gym all the time and got really buff, and driving nice cars and picking up young girls and hanging out at the country club all the time. So he was living the classic suburban, divorcé, midlife-crisis life, and I never resented him or thought, 'Oh, he's a horrible guy.' He was always really good to me and is really good to me—and really affectionate and really supportive of everything I do. But I just never wanted that for myself.

"That's probably why I did a lot of soul-searching early on, as far as what I wanted to do and sticking with that. And a lot of people I know don't have that, don't know what they want to do when they're out of college. It was just different circumstances for me, to at least hear what my calling was and follow it and never really get diverted."

Eric got a job working on campaign-finance reform, moving his way up the nonprofit ladder until becoming communications director of a national organization called Public

Campaign, making $23,000 a year. After that he went to work for New York congressman Jerry Nadler for almost four years, a gig he really loved. But then, way before anyone knew who Howard Dean was, Eric read an article "about this cute Vermont governor who thinks he can be president and—isn't it so funny—wants to run on healthcare."

Eric liked Dean's straight talk and got in touch with the campaign. The funny thing about people in politics, at least among those who work on campaigns, is that they don't *apply* for jobs like the rest of us, by sending out resumes and trying not to asphyxiate from the stress of waiting for feedback. They get in the car. They move to whatever city the job's in, and they start doing it. In Eric's case, he moved to New York.

The first few months of the campaign were exhilarating. One of Eric's first ideas was "Dr. Dean's house calls," old-school campaigning where the candidate would go to people's homes and talk to them about their problems. The house calls eventually evolved into house parties, where Dean would get on a national conference call to connect with people hosting simultaneous fundraisers. "Early on is really when I got most of my ideas out there. By the end, it was such a clusterfuck in the campaign that any idea would be killed to death in committee discussions."

But to let the cat out of the bag in a big way, Dean didn't get the Democratic party's nomination. And after months of working around the clock—I believe we shared bag of Doritos for breakfast during one Harlem campaign stop—Eric says he was "fucking tired." Nevertheless, he still wanted to be involved. And the day after the campaign ended, he started a website called Deaniacs for Edwards. "I got a huge amount of press for that, I mean, more than anything I got during the

campaign, because I was the only Dean person doing anything. Everyone else kind of fell off the face of the earth." The
Edwards campaign told Eric they would get the senator on the
phone for Dean supporters "anytime, anyplace," so Eric organized a national conference call and coached John Edwards
on how to talk to Deaniacs to get their support while being
sensitive to how raw they were from the loss.

"After that, I was pretty much spent. I took a couple of
months off and did nothing. I chilled out, woke up late, went
out and grabbed falafel or something, would dick around, look
at a newspaper, window-shop, go to a couple places in New
York that I hadn't seen yet, ride my bike, go out late, end up
staying up till like three in the morning." Eric was alone for
much of that time, but he says he needed that, because on the
campaign he was with people "24/7, with high pressure and
no time to think for yourself."

Eric, however, was running out of cash. He was living off
what he'd saved during the campaign. He probably could've
gotten a position within the Edwards campaign, but as he says,
"I really wanted to be true to the Dean supporters and not be
seen as a sellout or to be a sellout." Joining the Kerry campaign
was out of the question.

"Look, I can make a shitload of money—I got offers to go
to these big PR firms that do stuff for like HMOs and drug companies—[but] I'd feel dirty in a way. I want to feel good about
myself, so I can't do anything like that." Eric wants to do meaningful work. For him, remuneration is secondary. He says that
when he joined Dean's camp "the governor was going to be
an asterisk in the whole campaign and there was no promise of money." But Eric was inspired. The problem is that he
can't rejigger or determine how often a candidate who inspires

Politics is incredibly frustrating, especially being on a losing side.

him will come along. This puts Eric in kind of an awkward position, personally and politically, especially in terms of planning his life long-term. "Politics is incredibly frustrating, especially being on a losing side, and especially when you feel like you're getting beaten up all day." Nevertheless, Eric says he'll "always stick with it."

Jeff Shesol on Becoming a Presidential Speechwriter

As a member of the White House senior staff, Jeff Shesol served as deputy assistant to President Clinton and deputy director of presidential speechwriting, managing a staff of six. From 1998 to 2001, Mr. Shesol wrote about virtually every issue on the president's agenda, from global trade to the federal budget, from international financial architecture to information technology, and from economic development to the arts. In his final year at the White House, he coordinated the policy, communications strategy, and drafting process for the president's State of the Union address, of which he was principal author.

Before arriving at the White House, Mr. Shesol authored Mutual Contempt: Lyndon Johnson, Robert Kennedy, and the Feud that Defined a Decade, *a New York Times Notable Book. From 1994 to 1998, Mr. Shesol also wrote, illustrated, and syndicated a political comic strip,* Thatch, *which appeared daily in more than 150 newspapers.*

Well, I was not born a political operative. I took a pretty unconventional path to get here because I really didn't know where I was going. I had a good friend in grad school who said that his long-term plan was to have a series of really interesting short-term plans, and that's essentially been the case for me. There are a whole lot of different ways to get into speechwriting, and it's encouraging to know there's not one set way of accomplishing it. There are people who are journalists who have covered various policy matters—they became experts on one thing or another and were obviously good writers—who were interested in making the leap from observation or analysis to advocacy.

Another path that's a little more common for people who have varying kinds of political experience and a gift for writing—is to turn policy papers into the English language. That was one of the skills that was always in short supply in the White House and the administration, and it's always true in politics that there are a limited number of people who can actually translate wonky, abstract policy matters into language that is clear and, in a sense, can persuade.

I had a good friend in grad school who said that his long-term plan was to have a series of really interesting short-term plans, and that's essentially been the case for me.

You sort of think on the one hand that everyone can write, but not everyone can write a speech. It's a particular kind of skill, and some people have that ability more than others. When people discover that you can write a speech, all of a sudden you're writing a lot of speeches. So it's kind of a niche in politics, kind of a specialization, and it's more clearly defined than a communications job. It's a specific skill set, so there are a number of different ways to develop that skill set.

You have to have an understanding of politics, obviously, and it's helpful to have an understanding of history. You've [also] got to be a consumer of spoken word. You have to have an ear for it; you've got to spend time listening to it. Long before I ever considered being a speechwriter, I used to watch campaigns on TV, and I even covered them as a reporter in college, and then I would spend time on the phone with politically minded friends of mine and we would just take these things apart: "Can you believe he said such-and-such. . . It was totally an appeal to such-and-such. . . it wasn't even subtle." We'd sort of deconstruct the speeches. That was sort of one of the ways that I got into politics. . . not through going to political-science [classes], but through soaking it up and understanding how politicians talk.

It's helpful to have an understanding of history. You've [also] got to be a consumer of spoken word.

I was a student of American political history at Brown. My big activity was a daily comic strip in the college paper called *Thatch*. My senior year, it ended up getting syndicated around the country in different college papers. USA TODAY launched this thing in about 1990 called the College Information Network or something like that; they were starting a syndicate. I [sent] them my stuff and I got picked.

But a much bigger development [for me] was the first time political correctness was ever mentioned in a national paper. . . in a story in the *New York Times*. It was written by a Brown student who was a friend of mine. I had been doing some comic strips about political correctness and had created this character called "Politically Correct Person," this fatuous alter ego who was always crusading about what was right. My friend said, "Well, why don't you send one of your strips as an illustration of what's happening here?" So I sent them, and when I opened the paper on Sunday, not only did they run one of my strips, but they ran it huge — like the width of the entire page. And the next day — I'm a believer in the big-break theory — I got a call from a literary agent who's now my agent, who wanted to do a book of these comic strips; I got a call from a publisher who wanted to do the same thing; and I got a call from a cartoon syndicate, the first of a number of calls from cartoon syndicates.

Before I graduated, I ended up actually signing an agreement with Creators Syndicate in LA to syndicate some version of *Thatch* geared towards the real world. I had that all set up when I graduated, and then I went off to graduate school in England for two years. I had a Rhodes Scholarship to Oxford. I spent the next two years — while in graduate school — cooking up extra projects that I wanted to launch when I got back, and one was the comic strip. The second thing was the book that I wrote, subsequently. I did my thesis at Brown on the feud between Lyndon Johnson and Robert Kennedy and the impact that it had on politics and policy making in the '60s and beyond. And because I had been working with this literary agent on my comic-strip book, he wanted to know more about my thesis, and I sent it to him and he felt that it was a book. He said, "If you want to triple it in length and gear it towards a popular audience rather than an academic audience, we could really have a book here." So I spent the next two years at Oxford thinking of that, but not really doing anything about it. When I finished up, I came back, I moved to Washington, and Clinton was in office, and there was a lot of energy here.

I spent the next year and a half waiting tables and getting my comic strip started and also working on a book proposal. This took me about six months or so, and I got the book deal and then started to work from there. I took four to five years on this violent seesaw between doing the comic strip seven days a week, which during that period appeared in about 150 papers around the country, and writing this book. It was definitely too much to do at once, but I loved [the] two things too much to part with either one of them.

One thing I lacked, though, was that daily interaction that you have when you have a job with other people. Even though I had a lot of friends in Washington, I spent my whole day alone. Whether I was at the drawing table or whether I was [at] the Library of Congress, I was kind of in my own world. I started to feel kind of socially isolated. I was making about $35,000 doing the comic strips, so it wasn't too bad because I had some book money on top of that. I was supposed to take two years to write the book but it took about four.

I started to feel that I wasn't going to do the comic strip for too much longer; I felt like it was weighing me down and

I didn't know if people were reading it. It was just a matter of people of our generation weren't reading comics anymore because they just sucked. I was thinking about applying for a White House Fellowship, which seemed to be a way into the government. . . Ironically, one day out of the blue I got a handwritten note from President Clinton, who happened to have read my book, which was published that year. I was thrilled, obviously. Then two weeks later, I received a phone call from Michael Waldman, who was the chief speechwriter, and he said, "The President was reading your book and we have an opening as a speechwriter and [he] was wondering if you were interested in that." I was shocked and of course I had an interest in that, and it was a good time for me to make that shift. So I got out of my contract with Creators Syndicate, and I actually got my official job offer the day that the Lewinsky scandal broke. So I walked into the White House at a very interesting time. It is just a job that kind of dropped out of the sky.

You're expected to be enough of a generalist that you can write on just about anything coming down the pike, a process in which you become a so-called expert on something.

There were a series of interviews. I took a writing test, a speech assignment, which was something that they gave everyone applying for a speechwriting position. They would say, "Write a speech for Clinton to deliver at a dedication processional for [the] Martin Luther King Memorial on the Mall." They gave us a bunch of recent speeches written on related subjects [for reference], and we were free to call them and ask questions, and it was due in 48 hours, a typical speechwriting turnaround.

A speechwriter covers a couple of different beats. You may have an area, but you're expected to be enough of a generalist that you can write on just about anything coming down the pike, a process in which you become a so-called expert on something. You make phone calls, you do the research, and in [a] fairly short amount of time you can acquire the necessary familiarity with subjects.

Several Clinton speechwriters, myself included, all left the White House when we finished up there in 2001 and immediately started this business called West Wing Writers. President Clinton was our first client. If you can remember, he came out of the White House with a massive set of commitments on the lecture circuit. And he had so many speeches that he kept us very busy for the first 6 to 12 months, and that was sort of our startup capital because we knew we needed our revenue. Then we [began] to build our portfolio with other people. We actually got a lot of clients quickly because people we knew from the White House dispersed and went to lots of places, and when they got there, they needed the help and they knew that we did this, so we got pulled into a lot of interesting things. We always have new clients, whether it's a big project or a corporate merger or campaign. In terms of an active roster, we have a couple dozen at one time.

Harold Ickes on How to Stave Off Burnout

Prior to forming the Ickes & Enright Group in February 1997, Harold Ickes was assistant to the president and deputy chief of staff for political affairs and policy to President Clinton from January 1994 through January 1997. As deputy chief of staff, Mr. Ickes was responsible for managing a number of the president's substantive and policy initiatives. He was also an architect of the president's 1996 re-election campaign—which resulted in the re-election of the first Democratic president since FDR. *Mr. Ickes is also the chief of staff of America Coming Together.*

Look, each person's facts are different, but I think that campaigns are extraordinarily intense. They're almost unlike any other enterprise, especially a presidential campaign, because of the intensity of how fast they move, how disorganized they often are—at least internally. They often look organized from the outside. All of this adds up to an enormous amount of stress on anybody. It depends on people's temperament. That's why you tend to get a bunch of hyperactive loudmouths on campaigns. Putting that aside, when you think about the nature of a campaign, it

You tend to get a bunch of hyperactive loudmouths on campaigns.

is—as I suspect—much, much more stressful than most other jobs, especially a presidential campaign.

Then, if you lose, you are left with an enormous, enormous letdown. I don't know when [Eric's] burnout occurred. I don't know if it occurred during the campaign or after Governor Dean finally threw in the towel, but the only way of coping with it that I know of is keeping in mind several things: Number one, as important as the campaign was, it is not the most important thing in life. It's often hard to believe that when you're in the middle of it. And two, you just have to step back and refocus yourself. Maybe a thing to do is not go into another campaign, but to do something else for a while.

People who are successful in most things in life, and certainly in politics, are long-range players, and you really have to pace yourself.

Three is to keep in mind that people who are successful in most things in life, and certainly in politics, are long-range players, and you really have to pace yourself. It's easy to get totally wrapped up and completely consumed by the campaign you're in, but it's like running a race or like going through life—you've got to remember that there's going to be another week and another month and another year. You have to pace yourself. Those are the three things that I've relied on.

The goal is to try to get your candidate elected, and you really have to enforce discipline and pacing on yourself.

Otherwise, you will become burnt-out, and you'll become ineffective.

Even on a winning campaign—although there's the adrenaline of the win that kind of masks over your exhaustion—people are exhausted after it's over. It's an enervating process for those who are in the vortex, and people just have to remember there is going to be another day, another week, another month. And there's going to be another campaign. The thing I've learned the most is just pacing, and understanding that you can't do everything a campaign wants you to do. It's just impossible under the time constraints and the pressures, and you really have to prioritize. There are certain things you just say you're not going to do or that somebody else has got to do.

But because of the pressure-cooker atmosphere, there's a fanaticism in a campaign that's almost disorienting sometimes, which really takes a toll on you psychologically. People can become very depressed, or they can become nonfunctional, they can become catatonic. I've seen all manifestations, but I suspect—I'm not a psychiatrist or a psychologist—that they are due in large measure to the chaos. All of these things can lead to an innate frustration in people. At some point you just collapse—sometimes physically and sometimes mentally. Campaigns lend themselves to urgent do-or-die issues, sometimes by the hour, and the one that seemed most urgent to you an hour ago is completely superseded by the next most urgent thing, and often they aren't even that urgent when you step back and look at them.

Choosing a winning campaign is like choosing the right stock in the stock market. There are certain campaigns that are bound to win. All of it is odds, but if you want to get into a campaign that you think is going to win, then I suppose you look for a good, solid incumbent who has a track record of winning and who appears to be solid and safe. Those often aren't the most interesting campaigns to work in, but if your goal is a campaign that's bound to win, I would look at an incumbent as a best bet.

There are a lot of factors that go into it, and more often than not, everybody's wrong. No one would have expected Howard Dean to do as well as Howard Dean did. In November/December of [2003], if you and I had this conversation and I told you to bet the ranch on John Kerry winning the primary, you would have laughed at me. I think nobody expected George Bush to be put under the severe challenge he was put under. Now he ended up winning, but there really is no magic to this. At the outer edges, there are a bunch of goofy people who are never going to win anything, but the closer you get down to the center of what's real, the more difficult it becomes to predict.

Jason West on How to Win Elections

Best known for marrying same-sex couples in New York State, Green Party member Jason West is the 27-year-old house-painter-turned-mayor of New Paltz, New York.

After several years of activism work—organizing protests and boycotts, things like that—I realized that I was sick of lobbying. Because that's really what protesting is: a more dramatic form of lobbying. When you go to protest, you're basically there to try to exert some kind of pressure or influence on those who can make decisions, like the president and Congress. And after doing that for a while, I felt like I didn't have any power, I wasn't being listened to, it wasn't having any impact. So that's when I decided to really focus my energies on, instead of going to Washington DC or New York for protests, to really stay within our village and be more of a community organizer.

It took six years of organizing and building the Green Party in the village to get to the point where we can win elections. When I joined the party, it was four of us sitting around a kitchen table. And now six years later, we have 300 members in a village of 6,000 people, and we've won four elections in the past year. We've won the mayorship that I hold and three out of the four members of the board of the village New Paltz.

Mayor is a part-time job. I get paid now, but I didn't for years. My salary was just raised from $8,000 to $18,000 a year. The former mayor who was here was 72 and, you know, retired fairly comfortable financially. It was more of a hobby for him.

In terms of a career, it's not like you can go to college for this and then, you know, get a high-paying job. But it's much more fulfilling than any job I've ever had because I'm actually in the position of being a decision maker and I've been elected with my principles intact. I wasn't forced to compromise or sell myself out to win office. The people who go into politics as a career, I've found, are the people who are most easily corrupted because they just follow the money. If you go into politics because you're rooted in your community and you want to make good, or you want an effective mechanism or social justice and environmentalism, you probably won't get corrupted.

There are small elections that happen all over the country—city council, town boards, whatever. It's fairly simple to win an election. All you have to do is get more votes than anybody else. And you can do it with half a dozen people. Decide what you want in your neighborhood and get half a dozen friends together, put up some flyers. It's really just common sense. Talk to people in a relaxed way, you know, using common-sense language. Get rid of any jargon you might know. If you can speak with conviction and common sense about changes you want to make in your community, people are going to listen to you. Even if you don't win the election, you're able to bring up issues that otherwise don't get into the newspapers. Don't wait; don't let anybody tell you it's not the right time to fight for what you know is right and think long-term. And don't panic about whatever crisis of the moment happens to come up.

It's fairly simple to win an election. All you have to do is get more votes than anybody else.

The Aspiring Comedian

Ewwwwwwww," says Becky, scrunching up her nose in disgust when I ask her how she feels about the term *comedienne*. Right now, Becky, 27, works as a receptionist in a chic editing studio. But six years ago, when she was graduating from college, she wanted to become a missionary. When she didn't get into the mission-based program she applied to, she had to come to terms with the fact that maybe she wasn't cut out for the simple life. "I read these books about these intense people who go into places and live in a tent house and you only have like five belongings—two pairs of pants, two shirts, and a toothbrush, and I'm like, 'I don't know; I like clothes.'"

So she started working in a coffeehouse and performed in a "completely exhilarating" talent show there. She signed up for an improv class, which she says she did really badly in. "I'm a little bit shy and nervous, and when I'm uncomfortable I'm

not funny at all." It was around that time when her friends—
"part of them were my religious friends and part were not"—
performed an "intervention" where they asked Becky what she
was planning to be, professionally. (Personally, I want to know
who these know-it-all friends were who had their entire adult
lives mapped out at 22, right down to the last "and I'll wear
the pink visor and matching tennis skirt to the Seniors' Round-
Robin" geriatric detail.)

Nevertheless, Becky started doing standup: "I perform
pretty regularly, but at shows most people haven't heard of."
She says she stopped going to most open mics because they're
really tough places for women. Indeed. At a typical open mic,
30 or so standup comics will perform for five minutes each
and the audience will be full of other comics. As a result, says
Becky, they're not there to listen or laugh; they're likely to
heckle you instead.

"There have been times when I've been the only woman
at these things." She says guys in the audience will yell, "Oh,
you're cute," or my favorite, "I'd do you." One comic got
onstage and said, "By the way, we kicked your ass in World
War II." Becky, whose last name is Japanese, is like, "Are you
kidding me? Number one, I'm American. Number two, how
can you make fun of atomic warfare?" She says she's learned to
choose her crowds more wisely and that ultimately, you have to
do open mics every once in a while to bust your own chops.

Most times, she performs for free. When she does get paid
for a show, she pockets a crisp $20. Becky's been perform-
ing for three years now and admits, somewhat sheepishly, to
receiving "a lot" of financial support from her parents. "I could
live off my salary, barely—like scrape by, but I'm a spoiled kid
because I'm an only kid. I spend like a retard. Some people

drink. . . I buy clothing." Her parents gave her an ultimatum last year, at which point she started looking for a full-time job. "Up until now, I've had part-time jobs—some really bad ones," she says. "But recently, to the relief of my parents, I accepted a full-time job as a receptionist, and I can't help but think, am I taking a step backward?"

I visit Becky at her office during a rainstorm, and she makes me a cup of tea in a fine white mug in the kitchen. We sit on a leather sofa. It's cozy. I point out that she's allowed to read and send email all day, as long as she gets her work done.

Becky's parents sent her a birthday card this year an illustration of a bear skateboarding on the front under the words, "To a very special daughter." On the inside, all her parents wrote was, "Closing in on 30."

"I'm 27. The bear had a helmet on. They think I'm like a retarded bear skateboarding," Becky says. "I cried so hard because they haven't been crazy about what I'm doing, and I'm spending their money, pursuing something that's kind of lame and I'm almost 30."

Recently, to the relief of my parents, I accepted a full-time job as a receptionist, and I can't help but think, am I taking a step backward?

Becky wants to become a better comic but she also wants to please her parents—by being independent of them. Ideally, she'd like to tour with other comics and open up for bands. "I think I'm good and a lot sharper than when I started. I'm still a little scared by it all. . . . It's hard, though, because you see people that you know and that you've worked with before, and you're like, "How did that happen?" or "I wish I could do that."

Eric Drysdale on How to Become a Better Standup Comedian

Since 2000, Eric Drysdale has been a writer for The Daily Show *with Jon Stewart. While there, he has earned both an Emmy and a Peabody Award.*

I'm one of the many who got into writing for the *Daily Show* through standup comedy. I initially went into standup as a showcase for my writing, and I had the goal of being a writer the whole time. I started doing standup seriously in college, and then after college I was in Montreal for about a year. Because Montreal is a kind of smaller pond, I was able to work my way up a little bit, and in the course of a year was beginning to get paid a little bit, opening for acts, things like that. I was also doing various odd jobs that I hated. But I did standup and thought, "Well this is easy. I'll move to New York and do it in New York." And then I got to New York and it's not that easy. The clubs have this thing where you have to bring X amount of people. And you realize after a certain amount of time doing this that no matter how good you are, they only have a limited amount of slots to put the paid pros, and the pros don't get paid that much anyway. If they can keep the show going on a Tuesday night at seven o'clock that brings in as much as [a] prime-time show without having to pay the comedians, why not keep doing that? Why would you ever bump somebody up to the majors?

It became a drag because I'd just moved to New York City and I didn't have that many friends here, and I had to keep asking them to come see me perform week after week after week, and it's $25 a night and a two-drink minimum. About a year into it, I sort of knew in my brain that there must be better way to do it, but I didn't know of one at the time, so I just gave up. And then after four years of doing odd jobs and not doing any comedy, I got tired of not doing any comedy. I discov-

I did standup and thought, "Well this is easy. I'll move to New York and do it in New York." And then I got to New York and it's not that easy.

ered this indie comedy scene in New York, and found out that if you really wanted to, there were places to work pretty much every night of the week in the city.

I did open mics for three or four years. Open mics can be brutal, but there's no substitute for getting your jokes up in front of an audience, writing for an audience, getting into the idea that writing is not easy, but it's a part of the process. And you have to be unafraid of it. And not only writing, but rewriting. The only way you get that is by really listening and watching your sets. At a very early point in the process of doing this, a fellow comic said, "OK, you're taping your sets, but are you listening to them?" Well, sometimes yes, sometimes no. Well, listen to your sets; listen to where the laughs come. Sometimes you see people who do the same routine at the same open mic over and over and over again, but at the same holes where they're not getting a laugh—why aren't they going back and changing it the next week? Listen to yourself, listen to your audience. Then the same person said, why don't you start videotaping your sets? That's actually extremely revealing. Even if you only do it once every six months or so.

Eventually, from being out and about in the standup circles, I was brought on to a kind of higher-profile alternative show. And that led to a steady gig and a Comedy Central standup showcase. From there I had an opportunity to submit to the *Daily Show*. That was five years ago. At the *Daily Show*, our work schedule is different from any other comedy show out there because we're very reactive to the news. We're basically writing the comedy show for the most part for that day. We come in about nine thirty in the morning. The head writers and writers have a meeting for about an hour where it's probably a lot like any editorial meeting at a newspaper or TV news show. We decide what the top news stories are, how we're going to approach them, what the elements are of each story we're going to cover. So I have to come in with a full knowledge of what's in the news that day, which entails reading the newspaper and watching the news shows the night before.

That [meeting] usually lasts about an hour. Then the writers are kind of divided up among stories. At about one o'clock those jokes are handed in. Jon Stewart, the head writer, [the] executive producer, and a writer [chosen] on a rotating basis, sit down with the scripts that all the writers have written and pick the best jokes from all the packages. And then the head writer and the one revolving writer sit down and write the script from the stuff that has been picked. There's a rehearsal for the show. We leave at six o'clockish, seven o'clockish, to go home. And Jon is a huge part of this process all along the way.

Ryan Cott on How to Get a Booking Agent's Attention

Ryan Cott is the booking agent and floor manager for the Comedy Connection, a nightclub in Boston.

Every Monday, I think that maybe I can get the next big comedian coming in here. I'd love to be the guy who gave that person a chance to be able to do that.

For our open mic nights, it's a six- or seven-month waiting period, so I advise people to go to other rooms around town and work on other material. I want them to bring their A-game with us, and it takes a lot to catch my eye. The number-one thing for comics is being able to grab a crowd. And you should be able to do that within the first minute of being on stage. And that could be your signature because everybody should be able to do that. If you're going to be kind of a clumsy, silly guy, then go up there and say, "Hey, I'm a moron," and then go for a joke right after that and grab 'em with that joke. You can't keep the crowd guessing because you want to get them comfortable and try to relate somehow to what you're talking about.

What catches my eye is stage presence—how comfortable people are, and how thought-out their jokes are. A

The number-one thing for comics is being able to grab a crowd. And you should be able to do that within the first minute of being on stage.

lot of guys, they think they're funny around their buddies, and they'll go to the comedy club and recycle jokes and try to pawn them off as their own. That's absolutely the worst thing they can do. The only thing worse than that is actually stealing somebody else's jokes.

I keep notes on every comedian. I've got a couple people right now who I've bumped up a lot, started giving paid gigs to. You have to remember to be true to people. There's a lot of competition out there, and if bookers take care of you and give you gigs, you shouldn't ever sidestep them.

Marisa Ross on Why a Casting Director Is Your Friend

Marisa Ross has been a casting director for several years. Her most recent projects include World Cup Comedy, Campus Ladies, *and* Mindy & Brenda.

As a casting director, I'm a personal shopper of people. A director of production or producer hires me [and my partner] because of our knowledge of a certain genre of actors. I seem to be working a lot on improv-based comedy. So they hire me to gather actors and comedians, and my job is to bring them the right people, quickly and efficiently. Sometimes, I'll read something and have an idea immediately, who's right for it, or it will go to a named actor so no one will even audition for it. But for smaller stuff, it depends. When I'm doing a TV show, I only have a couple days of casting at the shows—that's it.

For TV, it's usually like six actors to a role that you end up submitting to the director. It really depends. Like, right now we're casting a pilot and it's long-term-based improv, like *Curb*

Your Enthusiasm. It's such a specific skill that we did a huge open call on a Sunday. We saw as many people as we could because we needed to discover new faces that could do that sort of thing. I would say that out of 200 people that day, we called back 4.

You're only coming to my office for an audition if I know you or if I've seen you in something. If you're an actress and you're just starting out with no manager and no agent, the only way you would be walking into my office is if I know you, you're a friend of somebody, somebody has recommended you, I've seen you in a play, somebody else has seen you in a play, somebody just saw you in a movie—you have to be seen. Acting classes are great too, and a lot of [the] time I'll call acting teachers when I'm looking for a specific type and say, "Hey, do you have any fantastic 18-to-25-year-old Asian people in your class?" Otherwise, you have a manager or an agent, and they submit the pictures of the people to me.

If you're a writer and you don't have anything that you've written that people can read, then how are you a writer? You may say you're a writer, but if you don't have anything written, then you're not. So if you're an actor you have to put yourself out there—I know a lot of actors who got together with other people to actually produce short films or put themselves in a short film to get it out

> **If you're a writer and you don't have anything that you've written that people can read, then how are you a writer?**

places; or they put showcases together. You can't just say, "I'm an actor, look at my picture." Somebody has to see you, and unless you're extraordinarily beautiful and you're Charlize Theron—what's the story with her, that she was discovered when she was standing in line at the bank? Those stories are like winning a lottery. If somebody just mails in a photograph, or a headshot and resume, if I don't know who that person is, I'm not going to take the time.

We get like thousands of submissions per breakdown we put out. A breakdown is an email that goes out to all agents and managers (and a lot of rogue actors who aren't really supposed to have it) that alerts them of a new project and who is involved and when it goes and what the characters are—what the casting directors are looking for. The breakdown will say we're looking for an 18-to-22-year-old wiry, small, nervous little boy who's really anxious because it's his first day of college. Let's say that's the breakdown, and so that's what we're initially looking for—someone who fits that image, who can act well.

But a lot of times we'll put that breakdown out and when we start auditioning actors, the producers or directors won't be responding to any of those people. Once we turned to them and said, "Hey, can we try something different?" We brought in this really, really fat kid and he was fantastic. That's who the role went to, which is not what we initially described. And there's this really, really good actor who I bring in for everything I do. He's a very odd-looking duck, but he gets cast constantly because he's such an extraordinary actor who makes all of these incredible choices that people are willing to change what the image in their head is of the role. But again, you have to be extraordinary.

When someone comes in my office for an audition, they have sides—two to three pages of material from whatever project it is of that character. So I read it with them, and either they're right or they're wrong. Physically, if they look right but they have made strange choices in their reading, I'll stop and give them an adjustment and say, "Try it this way." If they get it right the second time, they'll get a callback. If they don't, I'll say, "Thank you; great to meet you." Usually we schedule two to three people every 15 minutes, so the interaction is maybe 2 to 4 minutes. There isn't any chitchat.

A lot of actors come in and they're not prepared, and I don't believe that they really want the role. I don't like when people apologize for messing up and their body language says, "Oh, that sucked." Whenever I talk to actors, I tell them that auditioning is their job, that's what their profession is—much more than it is actually acting. Their profession is auditions because they're going to be auditioning for a long time before they get to the place where people are going to be offering them stuff. They should treat every audition like it's a performance. And if they don't like to audition or if they're frightened of auditions, they're not doing their job.

Treat every audition like it's a performance. . . An actor has to convince those producers that they should spend that exorbitant amount of money on them.

Basically, an actor has to convince those producers that they should spend an exorbitant amount of money of them. Like TV pilots—you're really investing potentially seven years into that person. They have to give such a spectacular performance. There has to be something about them that will make people want to watch. That's what makes people hirable—if they move you, if they make you laugh uncontrollably (for a comedy), if they scare the shit out of you (for a horror movie). Then there are actors who want it but are just physically wrong for the role because they want a beautiful blonde and the producers don't think [the actress] is pretty enough. That does happen.

A lot of times I tell people, "I really like you, but I just don't think you're right for this job, but I'll keep you in mind for other gigs." I'll get in trouble by their managers for it. Some actors try to fight me on it and say things like, "Well, I can change my hair." That's not the purpose of my saying that. The purpose of my saying that is I truly think you're interesting, but I don't think you're what they're looking for. So I don't mean it in a bad way, and when I tell them I'll remember them, I do. Even when people really blow their audition, I still remember them for other things because I know that people can have very off days. But I'm not the type of person to pat someone on the back and make them believe that they're going to get the job. It's just not up to me; it's too subjective.

My job is to bring in the best actor for the role and not waste anybody's time. So if it gets to the point where the actors in the room have an audition with the director, it means that I think they're special in some way—I think that they really should have this role. Casting directors are always viewed as these evil people guarding the gates, but really we're your best friends because we, for some reason, think that you should have this role. You wouldn't be in there if we didn't. The worst feeling for me is when I'm watching a session and an actor who I thought was interesting makes a horrible, unrealistic choice or is unprepared and just reads from the pages and never looks up. When that happens, I feel like I want to crawl into my skin and die, and pray that I don't get fired. Or when I see that somebody's really unique and special and I'm like, "Oh my gosh, this person is going to be a star, you should hire them," and the producers are like, "Um, nah . . . no . . . not into it." It happens all the time.

The Aspiring DJ

Talking to Mike makes me realize why I have so few male friends: I ask too many pesky, prying questions. But it also reminds me how well-suited laconic types are to turntables. You can go into the back of a dark room, set up the record players, and let the Body Rock do all the talking for you. Mike's a "meticulous, outgoing, friendly" senior at Indiana University, a Big 10 school with a campus population the size of a pretty big town. He spends his days studying graphic design. As for the rest of his life, he says, with characteristic economy, "everything is just music."

"It kind of happened on accident," says Mike, that he got into spinning, after a friend asked him to do it at another friend's birthday party. He compared the experience to being on stage with a band, because "you're controlling what people are doing, to a certain extent, and you're kind of in the limelight, but not really." That kind of limelight allowed Mike to trot out some of his favorite records—he's amassed "around 500 or so 45s and 300 to 400 LPs. It's not a totally huge collection, but it's sizable. I don't even know how many CDs I have."

He's done some more house parties, which he thinks are fun, but he's a realistic guy with more than a few marketable skills, and he's not going to faint with disappointment if this doesn't evolve into something more that a hobby. "I've only done one job where I got paid and they were selling beer or something, so I just let them pay me whatever because I was just doing it for fun. I think I got $15 or $20, so it really isn't that lucrative." He laughs. But he likes the idea of profiting from his hobby. The same way I'd be game to open a craft and coffee shop. Mike has a friend who's well-paid as a resident DJ at a club in Bloomington, which is about 45 minutes south of Indianapolis; so from that vantage point, the appeal is undeniable. It's also a good way to finance, in Mike's case, an "addiction" to music. "Basically you are being paid to play records and go buy new music which is, you know, pretty awesome."

Ben Harvey on the Radio

Ben Harvey is a weeknight DJ at the FM station K-Rock in New York City, the number-one radio market in the country.

Everything is determined by research. Basically, every week my boss will get a list of what order the songs we're playing are in terms of what people think of them. One song will be put in heavy rotation, one in medium rotation, and one in light rotation, and they put it all in a computer, and the computer sort of spits out a playlist. So I just get a list when I go in, and

I grab the CDs and I play them off the list. Usually I do some prep [work]. I subscribe to 14 magazines, most of them music-related. And I'll just go through and highlight stuff that I can use on the air, so I can say, "Hey, I read in *Rolling Stone* that these guys, you know, weren't potty-trained when they were little." When I'm in the studio, everyone pretty much leaves me alone. I just do my thing, talk five times an hour, and mess with the callers a little bit.

I was always told not to major in communications and to just go about your life by studying something else and then to just try to get hands-on work at a radio station. I majored in English at Brown. Brown didn't have courses on radio or anything, but they have a great radio station, WBRU. So I worked there, and basically I was on the air every day for four years in the 34th largest market in the country. After graduation, I worked weekends at Y100 in Philadelphia, and then they moved me up to nights, which was seven to midnight on weekdays. I did that for two years. Then I got a call from my current program director, and they needed a new night guy at K-Rock in New York. I've been here a little over a year.

Radio is one of the few careers where you really jump around from city to city because stations will flip formats based on ratings. DJs get bounced around a lot, especially in the smaller markets. Sometimes in smaller markets, regional accents can be good because it makes people feel comfortable, as long as it's the same regional accent as the region you're in. But in a major market, they definitely want a more normal sounding, middle-of-the-road accent.

Everyone when they start has such a "DJ voice." It takes a while to get rid of that and just talk like a regular person so listeners can relate to you. I mean, everyone has a DJ voice to a certain extent because you have to project to the microphone, but some people just take it to a whole new level where they just sound like such a cheeseball. I always wanted to be a DJ. I had a little fake radio station in my attic when I was a kid, which I called WBEN, and I would make fake radio shows and put them on tape. I think that helped.

In alternative radio, which is what I'm in, it helps if you have a sarcastic or cynical personality. If you're going into Top 40 or pop radio, I think it probably helps if you have a very outgoing, bubbly, I-love-life personality. In terms of potential employees, it helps if someone's eager and wants to learn and clearly has a radio bug. My bosses have always talked about how some people get the radio bug and some people don't. And I think people who know they have it will just know. And they will end up somewhere.

I think internships are really helpful. I've seen a lot of people start from interning and grow into overnight jocks and then weekend jocks. Some stations are now run by a computer overnight, which makes it harder to get into radio. [You used to be able to] start in an overnight position, which is midnight to 6 a.m., and that's always been a training ground for new DJs. But companies are cutting costs and they're automating that time slot. In smaller markets where they need to cut even more costs, they're either automating the

Some people get the radio bug and some people don't. And I think people who know they have it will just know.

time slot or they're importing voices from different places. But I'd say if you go to a station, get an internship, and find a mentor who can help you, it might take about a year to get to a level where you get on air, depending on the market.

DJ AM (aka Adam Goldstein) on the Scene

DJ AM *has produced remixes for Madonna and done scratches on albums for Will Smith. In addition to playing special events like parties thrown by Ashton Kutcher, Tom Cruise, and Beyonce Knowles,* DJ AM *is the resident* DJ *at the Hard Rock Hotel & Casino in Las Vegas, as well as Concorde, Prey, and Avalon Hollywood.*

How do you become a successful DJ? By doing every job you can, for whatever money it is. When you're just starting off, you don't say no. That's what I tell a lot of my friends who, already after a couple of weeks, they start getting snobby and saying, "Well, they're only offering me this." If you're just starting, do everything you can. Every time you have an opportunity to be playing in front of people, you should. I only did one bar mitzvah, thank goodness, and it was Steven Spielberg's son's bar mitzvah, so I guess if you're going to do one, that's probably the most fun one. But if someone's offering you a job

When you're just starting off, you don't say no.

or wants to hire you somewhere for anything, you should do it. And not only that, but the only way to get better at something—anything—is to keep doing it. Practice.

The thing is, practicing at home so much, it's kind of like acting—as soon as you get a crowd of people staring at you while you're trying to do it, it's a whole other world. It really truly is. Acting is a bad metaphor actually. You can get the technical side of it practicing alone, where you know how to do it. But you have to be playing in front of other people and seeing the crowd's reaction to see what works. There can be two records that have exactly the same tempo but a completely different sway to them—the way you move your body. Just because the beats match speedwise, doesn't mean it's a good mix. It has to have the same feel.

I played at my house all the time. I grew up in Philly, and my family was very rich for Philly, and then my dad went to jail. We lost everything, and we were really broke. I'm very grateful. I went from having everything to having absolutely nothing. If I had stayed—like a lot of my friends out here—with a silver spoon in my mouth the whole time, I don't think I'd be who I am now.

So then a friend of mine in LA, his dad opened a rent-a-car place, and above it there was a huge, huge storage space. His dad's rent-a-car place went out of business, but he still owned the property. So his dad let him throw this big after-hours there. We did it every Friday and Saturday. It started at 2 a.m. You know, in LA they stop selling alcohol at 2 a.m., so it's completely illegal. And we had a friend of ours who worked at a supermarket, in the stockroom, and he would steal cases of Budweiser and vodka, and we'd make these big vats of screwdivers or whatever, and that was what we sold. It was very shady. But it was weird because it turned into kind of a very Hollywood crowd with very seedy shit going on because the people had nowhere to go. I DJed there for $40 a night, and I would have to bring my turntable and my home stereo with its home, big speakers, and I would play from two to seven in the morning.

A lot of promoters would leave their clubs and note that everyone was going there, so they'd go there to promote and hand out flyers and shit. And they'd see the crowd's reaction to me DJing. Everywhere I'd go: "What's your name?" People started talking to me that way. Nothing ever came of it until — at the time I was working at CAA, the talent agency, in the mailroom — and while I was there, one of my friends was the assistant for one of the agency heads, and he decided to have his birthday party at Dragonfly. My friend asked me to DJ for him, at his boss's birthday party, on a Friday night. On Fridays they have a regular resident DJ, but I went and I brought my records and — because he was having this huge party with 300 people — they were letting him have his own DJ.

I got on and I'm DJing and these two guys just came in the booth and started staring at me. And I'm just like, "What the fuck are you looking at?" They were there for 10 minutes and said nothing. Then they turned around and left. That following Monday I get a call at CAA, and it was one of the guys from the booth. He said, "Hi. I was one of the guys who came to stare at you. I'm one of the owners of Dragonfly. Do you want a job Friday nights? We'll fire that guy if you start this Friday." I was like, "How much?" And they're like, "$150." I was jumping up and down, I was so happy. And that was my first job.

From there, I was very selfish for a while. I played a lot of what I played at the after-hours and didn't necessarily focus on the crowd so much as I did on my friends. Basically, as a DJ, you're there for the crowd. At home you get to practice, and you may work for a day on something just to get it to work. Let's say it involves a Joan Jett record, and then you could get there and it won't work. You know it's much more of a hip-hop crowd, and a pop hip-hop crowd, and they want Justin Timberlake and Beyonce and KISS-FM hip-hop. And you know what? You may just have to hold off on your big mix, because you're there for them. They're employing you. Your job is to please the masses. The majority rules, basically.

A rule of mine, personally, I focus on girls. If the girls are happy, the guys are happy, because when the girls are screaming and going nuts and losing their minds, the guys—it doesn't even matter what song is on—they're like, "Alright, cool." So I've always focused on the girls. Except I have my standards—I have certain records that are just so awful, and girls love them, but I just will not play them: Gloria Gaynor, "I Will Survive," and Pras, "Ghetto Superstar." I even get "I Will Survive," but it's just the most cliché, corny, cheesy "We Are Family" record ever made, and I can't deal. I just cannot deal with playing that. It like goes against my soul, musically. On occasion I get a girl who will actually ask for one of those, and I just look at them like, "No, honey, you're in the wrong club." But I'm in the position where I'm able to do that.

I was at Dragonfly for almost a year without getting any other jobs. Then one

Your job is to please the masses. The majority rules, basically. . . Except I have my standards.

night, there was some girl's birthday party, and I decided to pack up Jackson 5 and a little bit of disco-ish fun stuff, and I did it and everyone went nuts. When I saw that reaction, my arm hairs stood up. I thought, "Oh shit. I'm actually making the whole crowd scream, not just my friends." That opened my eyes to a whole new thing. So I started bringing a whole different set of records, and it started working. From there, other promoters started hiring me.

Now I'm the resident DJ at the Hard Rock Café in Las Vegas, every Friday and Saturday night, every week for a year. The travel is brutal, and I hate Vegas. I'm not a party guy. I'm seven years sober. I don't drink, I don't gamble, so I really don't like the city. But the people there, as cheesy as they are and touristy and typical—Vegas as it is—they really love me. They respond to me very well. They listen, and they're very into it. I'm appreciated there; therefore, I like it. It's better than playing some Hollywood club where everyone's so insecure and shallow and wondering what celebrities are there and how they look and who they're going to be able to bone tonight, where they're not even listening to me. They don't even care what's going on. I could turn the music off and they'd still be kind of moving and self-conscious. These people [in Vegas] just get drunk and want to party. It's like a big fucking frat party. So for as desperate and cheesy as it is, it's still fun, because they appreciate me.

I'm the luckiest guy alive. I'm 31 now; I don't plan on doing this forever. My mom always told me, "If you want to be successful in life, success equals happiness. If you're truly happy sitting in a dumpster, and you're in a dumpster, then you're successful." She also said that if you want to be successful, find what you love to do in life so much you'd do it for free, and get them to pay you for it. And that's what I did. I found a way to get paid lots of money doing the same thing I'd do for free anyway. You know, I DJed in my room forever for free, and now I get flown all over. I was just in Japan last week, Tokyo, DJing. I've DJed in almost every country. For private parties, I get up to $10,000. I've gotten $15,000. It's been a long time, about 10 years, that I've been doing these clubs in LA. So I've paid my dues. It's not like I'm an overnight DJ success. But I'm very, very satisfied.

Jo Maeder on Voiceover Work

Jo Maeder is a former New York City radio DJ. Her show, The Rock 'N Roll Madame, *used to follow Howard Stern. As a freelance voice talent, she records voiceovers from her home in North Carolina, saying things like, "Tonight on NBC Nightly News with Tom Brokaw" or "This ESPN half-time report brought to you by Harley Davidson. It's time to ride!"*

The local radio station had hired me to write commercials, and one day an account executive walks in and hands me $150. I said "What's this?" and he said, "Every time your commercials run on another station, you get $50." I didn't even know anything about voiceovers. So he said, "If you get in the union and you get a spot that runs nationally; you get all this money for residuals." So that's how I really started in the voiceover business.

Being the voice of a radio station is so much fun. I love it! I do "imaging voice"—it's the voice you hear in between songs. It's not the DJs you hear. And I'm saying things like, "Krater 96: Hawaii's number-one station to listen to at work." You're putting forth the image. . . the station-*ality*—that's a word they use. It's the personality of a station.

If you want to get into voiceovers, the first thing to do is tape the TV commercials you think you should do. Not just the commercials selling products, but promotional announcements that promote the TV show or the guy at the beginning who says, "And now it's *The Ellen DeGeneres Show*." Then you

You have to follow direction: If they say, "No, we want it more authoritative," you have to be able to do that.

need to tape yourself into a cassette recorder or whatever and then compare and say, "How well do I really sound compared to these people?" Ask other people, "How do I compare?"

The other thing that's very important is the inner clock. When I do my NBC stuff, they want it in 7.9 seconds—they don't want 8, they don't want 7.8—you have to know that. And versatility; can you read it in several different ways? And you have to follow direction: If they say, "No, we want it more authoritative," you have to be able to do that.

I think the best place to start is a local recording studio. So you have to find out, wherever you live, where the big advertising agencies and the big recording studios that produce or do post-production work on TV commercials [are]. Who do these agencies go to [in order to] record their commercials? Local recording studios are a great place to start. You can also go there to get your demo made. It used to be you only needed one demo. Now you need a demo for everything. You need a demo for commercials, narration, or promos.

The hard part is getting the work. If there are any casting or talent agencies in your town, you have to get in contact with them. There are agencies all over who will take on people in other locations, so you have to find agents—I know my agent in New York will take on people who have built up a lot of business. There are websites where "you give us $100 a year and we'll find you work." Most of the stuff is what we call "dollar-a-holler" stuff. They pay very little. Take a look at www. voicehunter.com.

When you get a contract, the radio stations typically will put you on a monthly retainer. A monthly retainer can range depending on your market size and if you're the primary voice. Typically the female is the accent voice (that's what they call us), so we don't get paid as much as the guys. But [retainers] can range from $200 a month to, in a big market, maybe $1,500 a month. What's so cool is that I sit here in my house and they email me the copy. I record it and send it back as an MP3. It's so easy now to set up a studio in your home, and it's not that expensive. It used to be you had to live in New York or LA, maybe Chicago. You can set up a home studio now for $10,000, which of course for a startup business isn't that much money.

The Aspiring Rock Star

Most of my aspirations are musical," says Kate, 31, a self-described "rube from Rhode Island" and lead singer of the band The Boxes. Kate's a straight talker with kind of a weird assortment of freelance jobs, "none of which are helping me on my quest for health insurance," which is, in itself, a crisis that is so very au courant.

Some nights she DJs in a bar for $150. Other nights she bartends for about the same amount. Ever since her dad—who's in a reggae band in Rhode Island and "smokes a lot of pot"—taught her how to play guitar, she's been in some rock band or another and is still trying to write "the perfect pop song." I think it's auspicious for Kate that she's open to a lot of jobs in music and not just the ones that enable her to travel with an entourage and rinse her hair with champagne to bring out its natural highlights. But she feels like she doesn't even have the fancy connections it takes to find out what cool jobs there are in music for aspiring rockers who are waiting for their star to rise.

Kate says she's been working in restaurants part-time for nearly 18 years—before, during, and after college—and that "there's nobody successful in my whole family." Two weeks ago when she was feeling pretty nervy, she quit her restaurant job (only to feel demoralized when she found out she'd been replaced within hours).

Kate's a straight talker with kind of a weird assortment of freelance jobs, "none of which are helping me on my quest for health insurance," which is, in itself, a crisis that is so very au courant.

She's been working as a fit model for chain stores like Aeropostle, where "the only requirement is a mind-numbing 'be a size 8.'" Samples are adjusted to fit her and then buyers watch her do stuff like bend over in them so they can see how they move. Weird, right? And not nearly as glamorous as depicted by Marilyn Monroe and Lauren Bacall in *How to Marry a Millionaire*, but still fairly intriguing when you consider that such a job pays her between $180 and $224 an hour. But it's not so stable, as Kate discovered when the company she was working for up and decided to start making all their samples in size 4 and told her her services were no longer needed. "I'm a bad fit model anyway," she says. "The whole goal of the job is not to change your measurements ever, because if you do, it will throw off the whole line." Kate would rather be able to eat burritos from time to time.

In any case, having quit the sucky restaurant job and been laid off from the mind-numbing cash cow, Kate's gone from "leisurely looking for a new and improved job" to "totally fucked." Kate says she's "scared of the office job" and that as much as she'd like to be a rock star (and she very much would), she'd be perfectly content with a job that is somehow music-related, even if it doesn't make her famous.

Adam Schlesinger on How to Know if You're Any Good

Adam Schlesinger is the singer/songwriter of the power-pop group Fountains of Wayne.

I was really lucky. When I got out of college, I did have some temp jobs for a while, but within a couple of years I was able to start making a living from working in music. At the beginning, I was playing in a band that was sort of a precursor band to Fountains of Wayne. We signed a record deal with a small startup label. That actually turned out to be kind of a big mistake, but at least for a while we had enough money to survive. The label went bankrupt and it actually took us a while to extricate ourselves legally from that situation, but at the time we were just excited to be recording and to have someone saying they liked our music.

Making it in the music business is one of those catch-22s, like a lot of things in life. It's definitely hard to get a shot for writing for anything unless you have some reputation to build on, but that's not to say it doesn't happen occasionally.

I was also simultaneously just trying to do any kind of work that I could involving music. I was going around and trying to meet people that did TV music and commercial music and writing stuff on spec for them or seeing if I could get small jobs doing that. If you're an unknown writer, nobody's going to just give you a job. You'll have to basically do the work and if they like it, then you'll cut a deal for it. Even now I still have to write a lot of stuff on spec, which I hate doing, but unfortunately there's no way around it.

One of the biggest breaks I've had outside of the band world [came when] I submitted a song for *That Thing You Do!*, a movie Tom Hanks directed and wrote, and they picked [it] and I was completely unknown at the time. Thankfully, they were confident enough at the time just to pick a song because they liked it and for no other reason. So that in turn led to a lot of other opportunities for me.

At that point I had a publishing deal with Polygram, which now is part of Universal. They had signed me along with the other members of my band Ivy. It was a brand-new band—at the time we got involved with them we only had one 7-inch single out. But that's a big part of what publishing companies do—they look for new talent and try to get involved really early so they can own a piece of it cheaply. You sign a deal with them, they give you some money, and they're supposed to be looking around for opportunities for you to write if you want to.

Publishing companies do different kinds of deals. Some of them are structured more around people who just want to write songs for their band and that's it. So they'll structure a deal that's based on delivering albums with your band. Other people get involved because they want to write for other things, and so they'll structure deals that are more about being a writer than about being a recording artist. Usually there's some kind of minimum number of songs that you need to deliver per year, and some kind of minimum commitment about the number of things they'll have to get played in order for them to continue working with you. So if you deliver 10 things and they can place a couple of them every year, and make a little money from it, that's usually enough [for them] to renew and keep going.

If you want to know if you're good, I think you can certainly go by other people's reactions. I found that if I wrote something that one person or two people thought was good, then it usually ended up that most everybody thought it was good. If you're in a band and you're just beating your head against the wall trying to get somebody interested in it for years on end, there's probably a reason why it's not going anywhere. It's probably not appealing to anyone. Whereas if you have something that people like right away, and is exciting to people, then it's probably going to be exciting to a lot of people. It's sort of about building up a lot of interest from a lot of places at once. That usually puts you in the best position.

I think you have to be realistic and you have to be honest with yourself. If you feel like you're getting enough encouragement from people to make you want to keep going, then you should keep going. If you feel like you've just been at it forever and nobody's responding to anything you do, then maybe it's because what you're doing isn't so great and you have to change what you're doing or try a different angle.

Two things sort of happened to me simultaneously that year, that was 1996: the Tom Hanks movie thing happened, and the first record from Fountains of Wayne was released. We got a record deal with a division of Atlantic Records. And the record did pretty well, and so those two things together helped me to develop some kind of reputation. From there it was a lot easier to at least find out about other opportunities, and occasionally people started calling me out of the blue, asking me to write something or to cowrite with other people. I tried to say yes whenever I could. I only had so much time and there were definitely some times when I made mistakes, when I said no and I should have said yes, because it ended up being a huge thing that I wasn't involved in. Even now, you have to try and figure out what's the best way to spend your time and guess which things are for real and which things aren't.

Chris Conley on Life on the Tour Bus

Chris Conley is the lead singer, songwriter, and founder of the band Saves the Day.

We started off just touring in a little van with four chairs and a bench, and eight or nine of us crammed in there. We didn't have enough money for hotels. We'd sleep on someone's floor in their basement. Sometimes our merch manager would put up a sign that said, "Saves the Day needs a place to crash." I've slept on so many concrete floors. I would wake up in the middle of the night with cat feces and cat vomit next to my ear, still smoldering.

> Sometimes our merch manager would put up a sign that said, "Saves the Day needs a place to crash."

Then we bought a 16-passenger van, which promptly broke down on an exit ramp in Baltimore, and had to have it towed all the way home.

It's hard for bands to get started if they don't have help from their parents, if their parents don't let them practice in the garage. We didn't even have enough money to run the air conditioning in the van. The band would make $50 a night, which would buy a meal for everybody, but nothing else. We didn't have a single penny for three years. It took us that long to get into the black. We were constantly touring, taking advances from our booking agents.

If we ever did get a hotel room, all eight or nine of us would have to sneak past the front-desk manager and cram into it. When we would drive around the country in the desert, we'd be in the desert and it would be hotter inside the car than outside. Those living conditions were so dismal. You're with eight other guys that smell. You can only afford ramen noodles and Taco Bell. It was only after our fourth or fifth U.S. tour, that I really felt like people started to come see us. But I learned that the more you get in people's faces and the more you come through town, by the next time there will be more people at the show.

It's really hard to go on stage when people don't like you, don't know you. I've had people heckling. People will say things about how I'm ugly or fat. I learned very early on not to look at the internet. When I was 18, after we'd just done our first tour someone said online that for Halloween they were going to dress up as Saves the Day and be a giant zit. I was a freshman in college who was living in dorm with all of these kids who were doing cocaine, and I was already feeling really insecure about random things that come with the baggage of that age.

On tour, we would start playing at 10 p.m., and be ready to go at the very earliest by midnight. We'd drive all night long to get to the next venue. One guy would drive until he couldn't stay up anymore, and then he would wake somebody else up and that guy would take a No-Doz. After a month of doing that every night, we were all dead. We were constantly spiritually drained.

Three of four years later we got a really good opportunity to do a tour with a band called Face to Face, and they offered for us to be on a tour bus for the first time. We had just gotten in a van accident that had totaled our van, and we [were] scared to death of driving—especially since it was a winter tour in Canada. On that tour bus, it was so nice, it felt like we were driving down that road in the Taj Mahal. It was really satisfying from our perspective, having been scraping by. We'd been eating cardboard noodles, and all of a sudden we're cruising on a bus and showing up at venues where they would have food waiting for us.

Eventually, we did a tour with blink-182 and Green Day, and we were playing venues that we'd never dreamed of playing—like Madison Square Garden—to a totally sold-out crowd. Getting to share the stage with my idols was beyond a dream come true for me.

These days we probably tour 20 to 25 weeks a year. Our tour bus now is a pretty swanky apartment on wheels. There's a lounge in the front with couches on either side of an eating area. There's a big TV/DVD player with satellite TV and video-games. All tour buses are different though—J.Lo, her tour bus must be way different from ours. There are 12 bunks on the bus, six on either side. We like to compare it to being in a coffin. If you're lying on your back and you put your elbow on the mat, you can reach the bottom of the next bunk. If you had a fear of being buried alive it might be terrible. And from your bunk, you can hear if someone else is snoring. It's not a good-smelling area, the bus, because everybody has sweaty show clothes. But it's not so bad. Your bunk is your only personal space, the only space you can call your own for two months on the road.

These are all the realities. People always fantasize about touring, this rock-and-roll lifestyle. It's not like Guns N' Roses.

I would recommend [being on the road as a musician] if you're passionate about music and if you love it, and if you're not meant to do anything else with your life. This has to be the only thing you want to do with your life in order to keep going, because it's a tough lifestyle. It really does get glamorized.

Mary Wood on the Unexpected Road to Jingle Writing

Mary Wood is a partner at Crushing Music and has written, among other things, the music for the Pepsi commercial that goes, "Ba buh ba ba bum, ba buh ba ba bum. The Joy of Coe-la-ah!"

My career took an unexpected turn. I started out as a singer/ songwriter. I came to New York after college looking for a record deal. I was tired of waitressing and I was lucky to get a job in a recording studio so that I could at least be doing something that was related to music. After that I got a job in the music department of an advertising agency.

Ad companies call companies like mine and will say, at one extreme, we have no idea what we want. The other extreme is when they give us a lot of direction—as in, the target is 12-year-old girls with tagline X.

The main thing I learned when I first started writing commercials is that you have to be concise. So you learn to express things in very few words. You only have 30 seconds for a hook, a bridge, and a chorus. And the ability to think fast—sometimes you only have a day, which is not a lot of time. Be open-minded to jobs that are musically related, like the music department of an ad agency or [working in] a recording studio doing voiceovers. Getting your foot in the door is the main thing.

The Aspiring Entrepreneur

We all fantasize about it. The "take this job and shove it" moment where you scoop up your bag, your rolodex, and in Alison's case, her Jack Russell terrier: "I was just in the shittiest mood, and it wasn't just affecting my 9 to 5, Monday through Friday, anymore." Alison, 26, was working at this hip advertising agency where the bosses went out drinking with the whole office every day after work.

"The agency I had been at before had a lot of bureaucracy. The creative director would never go out with a junior person, so I was really enticed by the accessibility. I also kind of thought advertising was sexy and interesting and a good place for people who enjoy creativity and writing." If you were a client, she'd talk to you about your brand and what you wanted it to stand for. And after three years in the business, she was making a salary of $40,000 a year.

The guy I worked for—if you take out the time that he was smoking pot in Europe and working at his dad's tennis camp—we had the same amount of work experience.

But after much of the staff at the still-hip-but-now-struggling firm was laid off ("nobody really knew what was going on or who was in charge"), Alison's creative job started to include a number of yucky and unrelated tasks, like analyzing weights of card stock for "point of sale" posters with vendors. Grunt work she would have been happy to do if she'd felt appreciated. But she didn't. She had a boss who seemed to take credit for work that she'd done. "The guy I worked for—if you take out the time that he was smoking pot in Europe and working at his dad's tennis camp—we had the same amount of work experience." (I love that.)

As the tension around the office mounted, things got worse and worse. Then one afternoon, Alison got "hauled into the back room" for a conference with her boss that didn't go well at all. When she started to tear up, he said, "Oh great, here come the waterworks," along with a bunch of other "really annoying, mean kind of stuff." She didn't want to return to her desk (which, incidentally, was located directly behind his). That's when she grabbed the dog. "As much as I would not recommend just walking out of your job, it was awesome to make that choice myself."

The upshot of being unemployed—after the thrill of going home, drinking a bottle of wine, and drunk-dialing everyone you know to tell them that you're finally free is over—is that nothing clarifies your thinking better about what it is you actually want to do.

"In a lot of ways I need to downgrade, shift to a lower gear, and do something that's more sustainable so I don't combust again," Alison says. She points to a friend of hers who's been in advertising for 15 years. "I always feel she's like the ghost of Christmas yet to come," says Alison. "Because her career is everything, she's single. . . that wouldn't be me. I was really lucky to meet my husband, but what's the point of having a great spouse if you work 10 to 12 hours a day in a back-biting industry?"

Like Melissa, the jewelry designer profiled in Chapter 5, it seems like Alison's personality is better suited to being her own supervisor. "It's not that I mind working really hard. When we would have new business pitches—the kind of thing where you work all night, doing the presentation at nine in the morning and going home at eleven to sleep—I actually really love that," she says. "The biggest problem that I have was the stress that I had with human beings at my job."

It's funny because for weeks before Alison quit her job, she'd been fantasizing aloud about opening a bakery with seasonal window displays

What's the point of having a great spouse if you work 10 to 12 hours a day in a back-biting industry?

and "really cool, homemade, authentic, delicious cakes that are made with love." Alison's good at making things like felled twigs into sparkling, forest-like installations. "I like to do a lot of things, like figure out how to solve weird little household problems and do things with my hands. With a store, I could be moving around a lot and not just sitting at a desk," she says.

The bakery idea has since evolved into more of a full-service café where people can go with their dogs and buy dog-related gifts that aren't schmaltzy. "I'd call it the Bark & Bite Café," she says. Consider it trademarked. "There are a lot of people like us in our town who don't have kids but are really into their dogs." And most pet-related merchandise, explains Alison, tends to be things like I-heart-my-dog aprons, "stuff that people with good taste just wouldn't possess."

It's amazing how much of who I felt I was was wrapped up in my career.

As you can imagine, Alison is way into her pup, who indulges her by wearing a variety of costumes, including bat wings, a crown, and a royal purple cape. "I used to carry him on the train and the subway in one of those pet pockets on my chest, so people know me as that crazy dog lady. I think the only reason I can get away with it is because I'm married. I imagine that people think, 'Oh, there really is someone for everybody. Look!'"

For now, Alison's sort of adjusting to what it means to be unemployed. "When I have to tell people about what I'm doing, second-tier friends who check in sort of out of concern and sort of out of voyeurism, those kinds of conversations are always kind of weird," she explains. "It's amazing how much of who I felt I was was wrapped up in my career. I find I only want to talk to people who I know really love me because I feel really uncomfortable, like maybe I'm going to be judged."

As a result, she's developed a strategy for describing what kind of a person she is to strangers. "I went to this knitting club in town and met some ladies. Everyone was like, 'What do you do?' so I said, 'Um, I'm writing a book!' I'd had this idea and had written like five pages three weeks earlier. Then I realized you can always be writing a book if you want to and nobody questions it because it sounds very sophisticated and exciting." Every one of the people she tells the whole truth to, however, envies her for having this brainstorming phase now. "Everybody needs a break," Alison says.

Sheila McCann on Transitioning and Choosing the Right Business to Open

Sheila McCann opened the House of Bread bakery in San Luis Obispo, a central California town, in 1996. Nine years later, it has grown into a franchise operation with about a dozen outlets scattered throughout the United States.

I was a public defender, which was something like a volatile love affair. There were incredible highs and incredible lows. The highs are when you really feel like you're helping out somebody or like when somebody was unjustly accused of something and the jury found them not guilty and they really were not guilty. The lows are when justice doesn't quite happen how you would like it to have happened—when you feel that someone was unjustly sentenced.

After one case in particular, I decided that I was going to do something else. There was a guy who had two little dogs and he dressed them up with hats and bandanas and sunglasses, and he put them in a red wagon. And he'd pull them around town and everybody loved the dogs, and kids would pet the dogs. That was how he related to people. He was a little weird—not scary-weird—but he couldn't relate to people in a normal fashion.

He got into a fight with the police officers [in his town] and one of them told him to put his dogs on a leash, so he stuck his tongue out at the police officers, who gave him a ticket. Then the man ripped the ticket up in front of the officers and things kind of escalated. One of the police officers said, "Well if you don't do what I say, I'm going to impound those dogs and they're going to be put to death." That's when [the man] lost it. He wrote threatening letters and dropped them off at the TV stations and the mayor's office and all of these places that basically said, "If they take my dogs away, then I'm going to off the next officer I see and someone's going to be a widow."

I was a public defender, which was something like a volatile love affair. There were incredible highs and incredible lows.

Threatening a public officer is a criminal offense. The chief of police got involved, and the judge got calls from the police officers telling them that they wanted the case sentenced to the maximum. I mean, it was a misdemeanor case—probation, seek some counseling, move on. That's what it should've been. That's what the probation department actually recommended. So I anticipated him getting probation, and the judge sentenced him for the maximum, which is eight years in prison.

When the judge said "eight years," I kind of turned to my client who was in handcuffs and he saw that I was upset and he tried to console me. He patted me on the back. He said, "Don't worry, I can do that time standing on my head." That's when I started crying, and I went in the juror room and he's kind of hobbling in after me, and the judge is going on about the sentence. We probably sat in the jury room until it was over, with my client feeding me tissues.

Once I made the decision that I wasn't going to do this anymore, all of a sudden this calmness came over me. Then I worked hard on figuring out what else I wanted to do. So I remained working for over a year because I wanted to save money to start a new venture. I decided that I wanted to go into business [for myself]. I thought about doing something else in law, but I didn't want to do something confrontational or controversial anymore. I just wanted something really positive. I wanted something that was the complete opposite of what I'd been doing.

At the time, I had saved up $103,000. Looking back on it, it was a lot, but I'm a simple person. I originally had a little over $60,000 when I had the idea to start my own business, and then I just saved, saved, saved and I cashed in all my stocks and IRAs. When you're young, retirement doesn't seem like it's much of anything, so it wasn't that big of a deal to me.

I had ideas for three different businesses and I researched each one. I went to a public library, and they have a business research center, and I came [upon] a book called *How to Start a Business in San Francisco*. It was by SCORE, the Senior Core of Retired Executives. SCORE is a nationally funded organization, and it's basically a bunch of old businessmen who help out people who are interested in starting their own business.

In starting a business, I think really the first major step is your mental step. That's what blocks people or gives them excuses. I don't have any children so it wasn't like I had people who were dependent upon me. So, the worst-case scenario would be if I opened up this business and it fell flat. Then I would owe people money. Well, I had once owed people $70,000 in student loans, so it wasn't that big of a deal to owe money to people again. I think that most people have a fear of failure, and I don't really have that. Mine is more of a fear of regret. I didn't want to be 80 years old and think, "What if?"

So then I had to figure out which business I wanted to do. I had three to choose from: [The first one was] a high-end sports retailer because I'm a sports person. People who have kayaks and bikes find that there's no place to sell them because customers are more comfortable buying things from a store than from other people. The problem is, you have to invest so much money up front buying all this equipment. Also, you can't hire someone for $7 an hour to determine what components on a bike have been changed out. Second was event planning. I really didn't want to do weddings—and believe me, I made the right decision since I just planned my own. Third was a bakery. I loved bread, and I looked into a franchise company and the response wasn't good. Long story short, I filled out the application, they told me I passed the first round, and I never heard back. "Forget this," I thought, "I can do it on my own."

I didn't want to spend six months at minimum wage learning the industry, so I talked to some wheat farmers who gave me the names of three or four consultants who had started their own bakeries throughout the country. You either have to learn the business or hire someone to teach you. Somehow you have to obtain the knowledge; otherwise, you're likely to fail. Most people make the mistake of getting into a business out of a passion. . . They like cooking, for example, so they'll open up a restaurant. But there's a lot more to it.

I rented a spot in downtown, a really nice spot. That's the other challenge: If you're not part of a franchise, landlords don't really want to rent to you. They want to rent to the Starbucks or the known entities. So when I first started, my landlord said no. So then I baked bread and brought it to him, along with a business plan. I also talked to the neighbors and tenants, and they went to the landlord and said, "She really has her act together; you should look at her business plan." He revisited the idea, and here I am.

Todd Woloson on the Importance of Consumer Marketing

Todd Woloson is the CEO of IZZE Beverage Company. A former venture capitalist, Todd cofounded the Global Education Fund, a nonprofit organization that builds libraries in developing countries. IZZE Beverage Company, which Todd cofounded with his friend Greg Stroh, manufactures and markets a line of sparkling fruit juices available at Whole Foods, Wild Oats, Starbucks, and Target.

I had no idea that I would ever care about marketing in my life. I mean, I'm just engulfed and impassioned by what I would term "a major inflection point in consumer marketing." The world of consumer marketing is changing right before our eyes. I just look at that as an opportunity. And what I mean by that is if you think all the rules are changing, what that ultimately means is that nobody is an expert. Which also means that nobody [is] that much smarter than I am or we are.

All the rules are changing. . . what that ultimately means is that nobody is an expert. Which also means that nobody [is] that much smarter than I am or we are.

The internet changed consumer marketing forever. It proved that it doesn't matter how much money you have; you can't buy a brand. I think [the internet] was permanently responsible for the unbelievable volume of ads and brand placements going around—all of these companies with all of this money trying to convince us that this is the next new thing. And I think the net result of that was consumers tend to filter through all of the advertisements, all of the advertising, in a way that they didn't before. I just don't think advertising works, is what I'm trying to say. There's a sense of skepticism. And ultimately, the internet has given us access behind the curtain. I mean, if we want to find out the real story, it's usually no more than two clicks away.

I think it's really exciting because what's required are real connections with people. You can't just sort of put crap in a bottle and support it with a huge multimillion-dollar ad campaign and expect it to do anything. I think that there needs to be real value, there needs to be a real differentiation, there needs to be something that people can tell their friends about and want to tell their friends about. And the brand is much more than the label in the front of the package; it's everything that the company does and says and how they act when they answer the phone. All of that is reflected in the brand. So I think it's an incredibly exciting time to be in the business, but it puts a lot more pressure on you. It can't be smoke and mirrors.

I've learned that a good product can mask a lot of mistakes. And ultimately, consumer acceptance is the only thing that matters. The rest is definitely rearranging deck chairs on the Titanic, so to speak. You can be great at opening distribution, you can be great at trade and promotions, and you can be great at managing production and excess inventories, but if people don't want it, you really are wasting time. Proof of concept is important.

I've also learned that having a product that is simple and understandable but also new is great. I see so many people trying to bend over backwards to show why something is so different. In consumer lines, I don't think full differentiation is required. I think incremental steps and some justification for a product being better is all that's required. But I've also learned the importance of focus—just sort of sticking on what you think is your opportunity. We've had a bunch of ideas for brand extensions, but for the moment we're just trying to ignore that and stayed focused on the project at hand.

Ultimately you don't know how much you're going to sell of any one product. It's a lot of best guessing. You can look at store volumes for similar products. But it's something you learn as you go. There's also the best guess, which is what you think might happen and then cut it in half. IZZE's been unusual in that we've exceeded expectations. But that doesn't happen very often.

I don't know if I'd consider myself a great entrepreneur, but I think that the biggest lesson I've learned personally is that you have to have an unwavering optimism, an absolute belief beyond reason that this is worth pursuing. A good idea is worth pursuing. What else are you going to do? Try to be safe? It never occurred to me not to do it. There are so many exits on this highway and it's so easy to back out. You need that almost blinder-like belief mixed with optimism. But at the same time you have to have a really critical eye of everything that you're doing, and detail really does count—that crossing the t's and dotting i's truly does matter. And it's frustrating; it's a little schizophrenic to be both at the same time, the unwavering optimism and absolute pessimism and skepticism and fear all at the same time.

There's a great misnomer about entrepreneurs being idea people, and it couldn't be further from the truth. All you need [is] one good idea; you don't need a bunch of ideas. And then you sort of need the opposite of the idea, which is blinder-like execution—you've got to get it done, you've got to keep moving forward. Ultimately, it's about an incredible amount of focus. The idea's just one part.

Mindy Weiss on How to Become an Event Planner

As the wedding planner for Jessica Simpson and Nick Lachey, Gwen Stefani and Gavin Rossdale, plus the ubiquitous Trista and Ryan, Mindy Weiss is almost too famous to be called an event planner. She opened her business, Mindy Weiss Party Consultants, in 1992 and is known for being discreet, creative, and detailed. But, not for nothing—she's also really, really sweet.

I was brought up with amazing, creative parties, so it was in my blood. My mother, for my sweet 16—I had no boobs and I was so upset that everybody had boobs but me—so she thought it would be funny if she gave my sweet 16 at the Playboy Club. We walked in and all the bunnies were wearing "Mindy's Sweet 16" sashes. The cake was a torso of a bunny. Now as a mother, if I ever got an invitation from somebody's child whose mother was giving their child a sweet 16 at the Playboy Club, I'd be mortified. But things were different then.

I kind of fell into the business because I started doing custom invitations. I used to do all the party planners' invitations for their parties. Then I did one party and it was like 375 people who said, "Who did this? Who did this?" It was amazing what happened, and I realized there was money to be made. And it wasn't hard for me—then. I thought, "OK, I can do this." And look what happened.

I always said, "I never want to be an event planner," because you truly have no life at all. You don't know how many calls I get: "You are so lucky! You have the best job!" Daily. I must get 25 emails a day. I had one email that said she was going to be [a] surgeon, but now she wants to be just like me. She wants

If you're going to be an event planner, you also have to be prepared to truly give up a very big part of your personal life.

to be a party planner, and I wrote back immediately and said, "Oh no, no, no, no, no. You have to be a surgeon. You have to. You can't do that."

If you're going to be an event planner, you also have to be prepared to truly give up a very big part of your personal life. You know how most people look forward to the weekend? I can't. That's the worst part of the week. You have to really be prepared to be at everybody's disposal 24/7. I work six days a week, sometimes seven. And it truly is probably the most rewarding job because I become part of people's life memories. But on the other hand, I become a psychologist, a friend, a mother, a sister, a boxing bag. Because everything comes out on me, no matter what the situation is.

You have to be a good problem solver—an immediate, quick-on-your-feet problem solver. And remain calm throughout everything. I think you have to present yourself with style and confidence because they're putting a very major thing in your hands. We do a flat fee, depending on the event, starting at $18,000 and going up from there. On kids' birthday parties, it's $250 an hour. On a wedding, I could spend 200 hours. On a party, it could be 100 hours. On a kid's birthday party, it could be 10 hours.

I always say that for someone who does not have experience but wants to really get into the business [of event planning] the best way is to work at a four- or five-star hotel in catering. I see all these courses online and all these certificates. You don't need a certificate to be a party planner or wedding planner. You need on-the-job training.

So say you go to the Four Seasons, and at the Four Seasons they do press junkets, weddings, bar mitzvahs, anniversaries—everything. It's just a one-stop shop for so many different types of events, and you are just on hand learning and there you can find out who the good florists are, the lighting, the bands, menu planning, wine selection. And then when you feel confident enough and you've stolen all the information that you can, it's time to go on your own. You leave. You make friends with your clients. You're planning their wedding. Even at a hotel, you start networking. You may have to do a few freebies and get your name out there, do a few charity events. It's a slow process. I've been doing it 18 years, and it's just in the last 4 years that I've been very, very successful.

My first celebrity wedding was Brooke Shields and Andre Agassi, so that kind of put me on the map. That was my first experience with celebrity weddings. They came to me through a friend of a friend. [Brooke's] assistant heard about me and came in with Brooke, and we hit it off in about three seconds. And I had no idea what was involved at all. I had no idea. So I learned a lot very quickly. Truly the only different beast is security and paparazzi, but otherwise it's all the same. All celebrities get excited just like any other bride.

The Aspiring Chef

I love grocery shopping. Love it," explains Jason, 31, as his awkward Great Dane Ruda Mae skitters around on her teenage legs. She licks the seat of the couch next to me in Jason's Los Angeles bungalow, which is almost completely hidden by the giant cactuses in the yard. "Must be peanut butter," Jason says. Ruda Mae sinks her head on his lap and takes a load off. Jason moved to Los Angeles from Denver, where he had worked at a sushi bar and a California-style fusion restaurant, so that he could pursue an acting career. "I like being onstage but [I've realized that I] get almost the same feeling from preparing food," he says. As his day job, he ended up working as a high-end travel agent for bands.

Growing up in Texas, Jason says his family sat for dinner together almost every night, which he says contributed to his love of food. His mother was a really good cook—though

Jason's father told him that she didn't start out that way. She'd grown up in a five-star hotel in England that her parents managed, so whenever she wanted something to eat she would simply tell the chef. Isn't that divine?

In any event, Jason started a catering company with his boyfriend about two and a half years ago. But that was easier said than done. "When you're starting your own business," he explains, "it gets to the point where it's time to quit whatever you were working on to pay the bills while you were building the business. But then you're kind of worried about going into the business by itself because you're not sure if you're going to make enough money at that point to pay the bills and keep going." Jason's boyfriend didn't want to make that leap, and Jason didn't feel ready or able to leap on his own, so the catering kind of petered out.

Though the boys entertain like crazy, Jason still wants to pursue food professionally. He wonders whether a restaurant would hire him as a chef based on his catering experience or whether he needs more formal training. He wants more training but is reluctant to enroll in a culinary school full-time. He fantasizes about opening a healthy home-cooking takeout place but has a ton of questions about determining how much food to prepare or how many ingredients to order so that nothing goes to waste. In the meantime, the Food Network is looking for new hosts, so he's sending in an application tape.

When I meet Jason and give Ruda Mae the green light to slobber all over me, Jason is preparing to cater a friend's baby shower. The menu includes coconut chicken with jasmine rice and mango, a Thai beef salad, and ahi tuna poki. (Poki, Jason explains, is a Hawaiian way of preparing fish. It's his signature dish, and it contains chopped raw tuna, garlic, macadamia nuts, dried seaweed, and spicy chili oil. He serves it on cucumber slices with soy sauce.) Jason cooks every night when he gets home from work. "Last night I didn't get home until eight o'clock. I had a bad day—it sucked—and I went in the kitchen. By the time I finished cooking and eating, I felt 100 percent better."

Jean-Georges Vongerichten on Creating Cravings

Simply put, Alsatian-born Jean-Georges is the most successfully creative chef in the country, pairing his three-star Michelin training with techniques he picked up in Asia. With an unprecedented total of twelve stars from the New York Times (including the four he earned at the very young age of 29) and an armful of awards from the James Beard Foundation, he is the rock star of the food world, whether you're a full-on foodie or just someone who likes to eat.

When I started in 1973, there were not many cooking schools. People went into apprenticeships, right into the fire. I went to work at a three-Michelin-star restaurant, and then I went to Asia for five years because the chef I was working with became a consultant. I was 23 years old; it was my first assignment ever. I arrived and went from being a line cook to being in charge of a kitchen with 25 cooks. It was pretty hard for me to deal with because my management skills were zero. It was a little premature for me, but I did it. Taking risks is part of cooking, part of living. Before my first chef job, the chef that I trained under said, "You can do it," and put all the confidence in me.

My first job, I came home crying some nights. My first job in Bangkok—my chef sent me over there by myself—I could not speak the language; I didn't speak English. I was taking English classes in the afternoon. It was crazy. It was 1980 and I said, "Well, OK, if I fail in Bangkok, I can always take my suitcase and go somewhere else." So I took more risks.

I'm still kind of that way in New York. I came with my suitcase and if everything corrupts, I'll take my suitcase somewhere else. If you know your trade, you can go anyplace. Now we have a restaurant in Shanghai, we have a restaurant in Paris. I travel a lot, about one week a month, and my first interest whenever I go to any continental city is to go to the market. There are great ingredients everywhere, and I can put them together differently. So I know I can go anyplace to cook.

As soon as you start dealing with other people, cooking becomes a different thing. I always say to people, if you want 100 percent of me, it has to be a counter with seven seats so that I can cook for you, wash the dishes, and serve you. Only then will you have 100 percent of me, but as soon as you start dealing with other people—a server, the maître d', it's only 20 percent of yourself. If I give a dish to one of my cooks, even if it's a very precise recipe, they're going to add their little touches, so you have to let go a little; otherwise, you can't work with a team.

We have 16 restaurants. Every day I wake up and think everything is going to collapse. I swear to God. Well, no, maybe not every day, but every other day. It's a fragile business. It's all about pleasing people; it's like art. My advice is simple: Believe in what you do. But that takes time. I mean, for six years I didn't know what I was doing. I was cooking the food part of it, but I couldn't come up with anything. It took me six years to connect; one day I said, "Wow, I can mix this with this."

In my kitchen, the young chefs with us, they have a harder job because I create restaurants, I create whatever I want to create, but the young people in the kitchen, they have to—whatever dish they have—they have to repeat it 25, 30, 40 times on the same night, the same dish, and to be consistent. Everybody has to go through that, I guess, to be able to do their own thing.

In the end, we create cravings. It took me 6 years to create dishes and 15 years to understand what people

If you come to a restaurant and the next morning you can't remember anything, then I've failed. With any business, especially the restaurant business, you have to be able to draw people back.

want. If you come to a restaurant and the next morning you can't remember anything, then I've failed. With any business, especially the restaurant business, you have to be able to draw people back. We have to create cravings to make people want to come back. Create for your public. Once you understand that, life is easy.

Dorothy Cann Hamilton on How to Choose a Cooking School

A lifelong Francophile and epicure, Dorothy Cann Hamilton founded the French Culinary Institute in 1984. Her distinguished career in vocational education and her outstanding reputation for innovative programs in gastronomy have resulted in numerous accolades and tributes, including the Chevalier dans l'Ordre National du Mérite and Chevalier du Mérite Agricole, awarded by the French government. Hamilton has also received the coveted Silver Spoon Award from Food Arts *magazine, marking her as a leader in the American restaurant community.*

Being a chef is a lot like being an artist, maybe even a fashion designer— it's something you know pretty much early on in your life.

Being a chef is a lot like being an artist, maybe even a fashion designer—it's something you know pretty much early on in your life. I don't think you would take an aptitude test and then find out you should be a chef. Nobody goes to a cooking school because they just like to cook. That's a different kind of school. They go to a cooking school because they want to be a chef or they want to be a food stylist or they want to be a food writer. They have a job in mind. Most cooking schools are vocational schools, so they have a responsibility to help place you in your first job.

Cooking schools are quite expensive because the equipment and the food to teach you are very expensive. There are a lot of costs in cooking schools, but if you have a decent credit rating, you can borrow enough money to go to school. If you do that, though, I can understand how anybody would want to be cautious. Ask, "What type of job am I going to get when I get out of this school?" Ask the school to show you their placement rate for the last year, where their graduates are working today. The school should have that record keeping. You should look and make sure that the school is licensed—better yet, that it's accredited by the federal government. Another thing you can do is call the state education department and the Better Business Bureau in your area and ask if any complaints have been filed against that school. If you're going to make this kind of investment, you're really going to have to do your homework before you go.

There are a lot of questions that people should ask when they're looking at a cooking school. One is, "What is the curriculum?" You don't want to go to a school where they just throw a chef in the classroom and say, "Teach." You may not get a well-rounded education on everything because perhaps they didn't like doing fish sauté or something like that, or they're not particularly good in pastry so they don't bother with that either. You should look for a school that has an established faculty with chefs who have been trained specifically for teaching.

The other thing you have to look into is the backgrounds of the teachers, as chefs. The difference between a good and a great restaurant is a lot of finesse and understanding the subtleties and its little things. Anyone can teach you how to hold a knife. It's from the very first day; it's learning the attitude, it's learning how to use your eyes and your nose and getting your basic training from the very best, which is so important.

Aside from the teachers, their background, and their personal communication skills and teaching background, I think you have to look at how well equipped the school is. Do they use really good equipment, or are you going to be hampered by using mediocre equipment that breaks down or is not professional equipment that you would find in a real kitchen when you go out to work? You can really tell how good a school is when you look at the ingredients used. Do they buy cheap meat so no matter how you cook it, it's never going to taste good? Are you going to learn lobster or are you going to cook chicken all the time? When you frost a cake, are they going to give you real cake, or are you going to use styrofoam? How organized is the school; how clean is the school? Do they have one dishwasher? Kitchens have to be spotless, and that's part of your training; it's learning about that cleanliness. So if you go in and [the kitchen] looks rough and tumble, you're not going to be getting a very essential part of chef training.

Even if you're going to stay in cooking school in the United States, you should try in your life to take vacations abroad and eat abroad because it will stimulate your imagination and make you a much more profound cook. It just opens up your eyes and your taste buds. Culturally, the way people eat is different everywhere in the world. That being said, there are some real reasons, if you are going to be a professional, to learn in the United States. One, the equipment is different. Two, the products are different—it's very hard for a European to come over here and make pastry or bread because the flour is so different. Three, American taste buds are different. In America, even at the French Culinary Institute, we serve much larger portions than they would ever serve in France. So if you're going to look to ever be a professional, there are a lot of reasons to learn in the vernacular here what you can do.

When you get out of cooking school, usually the best jobs pay the least money. There are people who would go work for free for chefs like Jean-Georges, so they don't have to pay a lot to their entry-level workers. It really depends what kind of job you're looking for, but any entry-level job is not going to be highly paid. I think it can be anywhere from $18,000 to $30,000 for a first job, depending on where you want to go and what you want to do. But quite quickly, one year to two years after that, it ramps up dramatically. We did a survey a number of years ago and [found that] 5 years out, our average student was making $40,000 a year, and 10 years out, they were making over $75,000 in executive-chef positions. An entry-level position would be a cook. It doesn't sound glamorous, but there's a difference between a short-order cook and a professional cook who is going into a real operation and starting up the career ladder.

You should try in your life to take vacations abroad and eat abroad because it will stimulate your imagination and make you a much more profound cook. It just opens up your eyes and your taste buds.

A cook will come in and the first thing they have to do is get their station ready, which is called *mise en place*, French for "put in place." You get all your seasonings out, get all of your knives out. You get your cutting boards, your towels, and you get yourself ready. Then you get all your products. In a way, a kitchen is set up very militaristically; there are stations. *Chef*, you know, means "chief," and the executive chef is the general. After that, you have the sous-chef, which is the captain, and then you have the meat station, the dessert station, and the appetizer/salad station, and then you'll have a chef at each of those stations with their lieutenants. Under them are the sergeants and privates doing the work.

So if you come in, you are the private; so you're going to get the grunt work, like peeling the carrots, cleaning the fish, seasoning the fish, getting ready for the lieutenant in that area to sauté it all. Then you're going to start working up that ladder—making dough, preparing in the pastry kitchen making tarts, putting whipped cream on top of things. Depending on the size of the kitchen, an executive chef would or wouldn't do the cooking. An executive chef in a small kitchen would, but an executive chef at a large hotel is what we call a "pencil chef." He's got thousands and thousands of people to feed and [is] just organizing the labor pool, doing the food ordering, making the menus, checking in that it's all going out, and tasting it. He doesn't have time; he couldn't possibly cook.

Hannah Sweets on Starting at the Bottom

Hannah Sweets was a professional ballet dancer with the Des Moines Ballet, Dallas Black Dance Theater, Alvin Ailey American Dance Theater, and Donald Byrd/The Group during a 15-year period. When she switched courses entirely in pursuit of a career as a chef, she started in prep and worked her way up to sous-chef at several of Dallas's fine restaurants. She is now the executive chef at a high-end bed-and-breakfast in Texas hill country.

Food, to me, is the same kind of discipline that dance is. You're on your feet for long periods of time, it can be physically grueling, there's a whole lot of sweating. But with food, the end product is more tangible. I can see, feel, and taste and touch what I create as opposed to waiting for somebody else to tell me the value of my own work. I was not realizing my own potential when I was dancing. That was much clearer to me when I was cooking. And I mean, what's better than food?

I was 26 when I decided that I was going to stop dancing, that my body couldn't take it anymore, and that it was too emotionally draining for me. My mother's a writer, and she was doing a feature on a Victorian bed-and-breakfast in Cape May, New Jersey. I was depressed and I wasn't really sure what I wanted to do with my life, so I went down for the weekend with her to just relax. By the end of the weekend, I was working in the kitchen. I started out as a prep cook and by the end of the summer they had promoted me to a kitchen-manager position.

I'd always worked, you know, in restaurants when I was dancing, either waiting tables or bartending or some aspect of food and beverage. I had done some catering work. And I don't think I'd realized it completely by then, but I think I'd already decided that I would be a chef.

I moved down to Dallas to be closer to my mother, and this restaurant chain was opening a new mock-Cuban restaurant called the Samba Room. I just walked in, interviewed, started working as a garde-manger [French term for the area where cold dishes are prepared] cook—your appetizers and salads. I mean, I started at the bottom. And I was promoted after about six months, to a saucier, the person who takes care of all the sauces. Then I left Samba Room to work at the Mansion on Turtle Creek. At the time, it was Dallas's only five-star restaurant. And I was working private dining there—banquet. I was there for almost two years, doing almost everything.

Food is the same kind of discipline that dance is. You're on your feet for long periods of time, it can be physically grueling, there's a whole lot of sweating.

The chef for whom I was working was in and out of the restaurant quite a bit, so a lot of responsibility landed on my shoulders. I was a lead cook for him for private banquets and press dining. We did a lot seven-course wine dinners, very nice meals.

After the Mansion, I went to work at the Adolphus, a French restaurant. I was working as a pastry cook, for not very long. Pastry wasn't my cup of tea, and the pastry chef at the time was a real misogynist. [Then] I went to work for a family as their personal chef. That was depressing. The guy that I worked for didn't like cilantro; didn't like garlic; didn't like bell peppers, onions, garlic; didn't drink — the list of things he didn't like went on for so long that it just became really disappointing to cook for him. He was on an Atkins diet too, so I made salad and meat. I wasn't creating. And I didn't have any soundboards either. There's a camaraderie in the kitchen that you get used to, that you become almost addicted to, and it's definitely not there when you don't have cooks or any kind of service staff.

There's a camaraderie in the kitchen that you get used to, that you become almost addicted to.

The last job that I had I was working at [the restaurant] NANA in Dallas. That was by far my favorite job, and I was there for almost three years. The people that I worked with, the food we were creating, the chef for whom I worked, it was just a combination that is very rarely found. It was a good education for me. And my boss introduced me to the owner [of] the restaurant I work for now. She was a friend of his family's. She decided to open a B&B in Fredericksburg and she was looking for a chef and David recommended me, and we met and we totally fell in love and that's history.

Now I'm an executive chef, and it's not as easy or pretty or glamorous as everybody thinks it is. It's a lot of hard work. It's a lot of long hours. You take full responsibility for the food. You are responsible for whom, with whom, you work. You're responsible for making it happen. You're also responsible for taking care of food costs. And with the opening [of] this new restaurant, I was doing drywall and a lot of things that you don't think about when you're making a new restaurant—like spacing floor drains and the ergonomics of a kitchen, how it's going to flow, how it's going to work. You have to think about things like that.

You can become a genuinely talented chef without having gone to culinary school, but then again there are lots of things that I wish that I had the opportunity to learn. I would like to travel. I think the best way to learn is to get out of America, to go to Europe, go to Asia, discover other cuisines, to be open-minded, to explore. I don't think anybody ever stops learning and I think that the true learning begins, you know, the last day of school when you start working in a kitchen.

A headhunter found me for the personal-chef position. The other jobs, I just walked in and said, "I'm here and I want a job." I found myself to be infinitely more fearless than I was when I was dancing. If you want to be a chef, don't be afraid. Have confidence in what you do. Believe in your product and never, ever skimp on the quality. I mean that across the board: Don't skimp on quality of life for yourself, and don't skimp on quality of product or whatever you're presenting. You're going to be living it, you're [going] to be breathing it, so you better love it. About a third of it when you start is talent and the rest of it is being able to really hear what chefs are telling you, working cleanly and efficiently, and to pay attention—to listen, to learn, to watch. Watch everything going on around you. Be a part of all of it. Just stay strong; it always gets better. And at the end of the day, you will never be hungry.

The Aspiring Writer and Editor

Every June, I look forward to meeting the new crop of the American Society of Magazine Editors' summer interns. ASME is the magazine industry's professional association and watchdog organization. They are the ones who bestow the industry's highest honors and come up with the industry's rules, like dictating that ads resembling articles must say "Advertisement" at the top of the page.

For someone interested in publishing, being an ASME summer intern is about as good as it gets. For one thing, you get paid to work at a magazine and are given real editorial duties, like fact checking and writing small items. On top of all that, ASME organizes all these special events and programs for you, like lectures from editors in chief, cocktail parties at

Newsweek, tours of the *New Yorker* or *Rolling Stone* offices, and luncheons at the Princeton Club. It's like being in *The Bell Jar*, without all the craziness.

I was an ASME intern when I was in college. My favorite session of the summer was listening to Richard Stolley describe how he acquired the Zapruder film of President Kennedy's assassination for Time Life. He was a graceful and modest speaker and left us with the impression—deliberately, I think—that his manners and the fact that he was polite to Abraham Zapruder's secretary helped him seal the deal, even though other news organizations were offering more money for the footage. I don't have any stories of historical significance myself, but I am often invited to be a panelist for an ASME session called "The Path from Your Internship to Your First Job."

As far as panels go, this one tends to be fairly rowdy. One of the editors, for example, has this very funny, deadpan delivery in describing how she's always threatening to leave magazines to become a cop. Ironically, we also talk a lot about manners and the importance of thank-you notes. Old-fashioned ones on paper. You'd be surprised how rarely anyone sends them.

It's like being in *The Bell Jar*, without all the craziness.

I often meet with college students over a cup of tea in our company cafeteria. Start in newspapers, I tell them, to build your skills and alacrity. Learn how to write and to think and to speak by studying the classics—you'll pick up the journalism business on the job. You can count the number who have sent me notes afterwards because they fit on one small panel of my office bulletin board. The other thing we go on about during the panel is how important it is to follow up and be cheerful—and to show that you're not only *not* averse to grunt work, but eager to do it as an entry-level assistant at a magazine.

It was after one such panel that I met Megan, age 22. Of the two types of people that bum rush panelists after a session like this—the outwardly ambitious ones who want to pitch you stories, and the ones who are obviously summoning all their available courage and some of their reserves to introduce themselves to a total stranger—Megan fell into the latter camp. I, myself, belong to that camp too. So I liked her immediately.

As a general rule, I tend to favor the underdog. Not the intellectual underdog, but the one who doesn't come from a fancy family and who has to rely on diligence and pluck to get her first job. Megan is exactly this kind of a girl, and she presents herself as sweet and curious. Even in that first meeting, while we washed our hands side by side in the women's restroom, she confessed to feeling self-conscious about being the student from SUNY-Plattsburgh among kids from

> I tend to favor the underdog. Not the intellectual underdog, but the one who doesn't come from a fancy family and who has to rely on diligence and pluck to get her first job.

Northwestern and Yale. We had a cup of coffee together. In that order, if you care.

After that encounter, Megan started to send me updates via email, often using the heading "ASME stalker girl." I love reading them because they're about adventures like surprising and appalling herself by spending too much money on a sundress, celebrating her birthday in the kind of dive bar where you discard peanut shells on the floor, and how frustrated she gets working in retail at the mall in upstate New York. In her words, "A person can only fold so many shirts and be nice to so many snotty preteens before she's ready to snap and take them out with a mannequin."

Even with all her experience—in addition to her ASME summer internship, Megan's been the editor in chief of an online magazine for three years—she's worried about finding a job. She spends a lot of time obsessing over cover letters. "With magazines, there are 400,000 people just like me, just as qualified as me. God knows, that's probably a low-ball figure," she says. At networking events, she's met "motivated, focused [people] just trying to make enough money so they can afford to keep interviewing for, like, three years."

I try to reassure her by telling her the only truth I know, which is that every wonderful intern I've known—I only keep in touch with the wonderful ones—has found a full-time, entry-level job within a few months of graduating. Ultimately, it's the sum total of all the little things that make you want to shake the bushes on behalf of an aspiring writer or magazine editor. Megan made an impression in her own way: with earnest enthusiasm. She never made me feel finessed. As a result, I'd be honored to help her and ask other editors I know to do the same. It's worth it, just to receive one of her well-written and utterly charming thank-you notes.

Laurel Touby on How to Be a Freelance Writer

Laurel Touby founded mediabistro.com in 1997, and since then this community of media professionals has grown to more than 500,000. mediabistro.com hosts more than 200 events for media professionals around the country each year and offers more than 100 classes around the country and online.

Let's say you write kickass letters. Everyone tells you, "You have a way with words." Because that's basically how all of us start in freelancing. At some point in a writer's life, someone has told him or her, "You have a way with words; you should really consider being a writer or writing something." But there are some things you really should learn about writing. One is it's not always going to be what [you] imagined in your wildest dreams that it'd be. So when you sit there and write your blog or your letter or poetry, you're able to go to the furthest extent of your creativity with no repercussions, no one not paying you because of it, nobody rejecting your work.

Basically you have to make a decision: Do I want to be a journalist, or do I want to be a writer? Because they are two different things. The way you can reach that decision, whether you want to be a writer or a journalist, is going online and doing some articles, actual journalism. Or if you really have the confidence and think you can get paid for it, channel your time and effort and energy to a local newspaper, to a trade magazine in your industry, to [a] local-community-kind-of-thing or a nonprofit organization that has a newsletter or magazine. Or contact your alumni association or publication. Those are all great places to get started, either paid or unpaid.

You have to make a decision: Do I want to be a journalist, or do I want to be a writer? Because they are two different things.

If you can wrangle some money [out] of it, more power to you. But most of the time, it's going to be hard if you have no track record and no clips. This is your way to make clips. This is what I did—I went out to a small local paper and I said, "I have no clips since college." I was three years out of school, and they thought, "OK, we'll try you out with something, but we're not going to pay you for it." Or, "We'll pay you $25 if it we run it." So I went to a gay pride parade in Brooklyn. They liked it and they ran it, and they let me do a couple more assignments.

Then what I did was called up every single person who'd gone to my school, Smith College, who was either a writer or editor and said, "How do I become you?" It's what's called an "informational interview." If you're changing careers, you can call nearly anybody in the world and ask them how they got to where they got. And people love talking about themselves, they love talking about their career paths, and most people like helping other people. So unless you're calling the secretary of state [people will talk to you].

The deal is you call up and say, "I'm switching my career. I think I have some really great skills in that area, but I'd love to know how you did what you did. I'd like 15 minutes of your time, over the phone or over coffee if you'd let me. I'll buy coffee. And I just want to pick your brain about eight questions that I have, just eight questions." And then you're limited to those eight questions, and those better be damn good questions. And you better let that person go at the end of your eight questions so that they don't feel like you're abusing your time period with them.

And then you should follow up with that person later on—that's the key. Following up later with, "You convinced me that I should pursue this career, and I would like to do it the way you did it, by working first at a blah blah blah type of publication. Could you perhaps turn me on to some people you might know at such-and-such publication. Here is. . . " It has to be very targeted, very direct, very aggressive without being pushy about your needs and your desires and your skills. The worst thing you can do is have that great interaction with that great person and then let it drop and never talk to them again.

The scaredy-cats are the ones who don't do this career. The people who have any boldness or any sense of self-worth are the ones who do this career. You have to reach out to the community and meet people like you and live in a neighborhood where there are people like you. Coming to a place like New York—people say it's too expensive or too much—but it's better to be here. You hear about more stuff, you stay connected more, you meet people who are doing what you're doing and it inspires you.

Once you've gotten some clips under your belt—and it's going to take some time, three to six months at least, because changing careers takes time, anytime you do it. And this is an exceptionally hard career to change into because it's a talent career. It's all about talent and glamour and there are so many people trying to get in to it. So once you've start getting those clips together, you've got to start working your way up to the next level of assignment. Whether it's the same publication you've worked for, [doing] bigger, better assignments. Or whether you try to tackle a new venue.

And the other thing you have to decide at this point is, now that I want to be a journalist, is there any type of area I want to specialize in? Because you can make a much better living, much easier, if you specialize in something. Especially if you specialize in something that nobody else wants. Let's put it this way, everybody wants to be a travel writer, everyone wants to be in fashion, everybody wants to be at a women's magazine, men's magazine. There are just hordes of people trying to get in to those. [Instead] you try to get in to something that nobody knows very well, or that nobody wants.

Let's say you've been working in retail, you know a little about retail, you know a bit about fashion. Let's say you've been working there and you noticed a trend, like kids coming in and buying a certain type of item. Well, sell that, sell that expertise to *Women's Wear Daily*. Don't go to *Glamour*; start out at WWD, start out at a trade, start out at a place that you're going to get there a little bit faster. Pitch your expertise or some observation that you've made because you're so close to your industry, and you're so observant of the trends in your own particular industry. And take that and turn that into something, leverage that into a start at a trade—or a glossy if you can. If you're reading this chapter, supposedly you have this ability and you already have this expertise and this knowledge. So leverage that into freelance writing. That's really a good way to break in.

I don't think editors read all the pitch letters they get, but they read them enough. It's not like the book industry, where you have a huge slush pile. If you write something that's short and to the point and says, "I can give you more information if you're interested. I've written for other publications. I can tell you more about myself." And then you follow up—not just send it and hope and pray. You've got to follow up: "Give me a call at this number if you need me sooner; I can turn this around quickly."

Be persistent as all hell, without being rude. And realize that this is going to hurt, it's going to be a process, and it's going to take 100 pitches before you get an assignment.

Another thing you want to do is pitch stuff to newspapers. They don't pay as much but they have a fast turnaround time and they have a lot more space to fill. Editors might be curt and rude, but it's not personal at all. You've got to think like the best of salespeople—you've got to keep going at it. And be persistent as all hell, without being rude. And realize that this is going to hurt, it's going to be a process, and it's going to take 100 pitches before you get an assignment. If you go out in there thinking, "This is going to take me 100 pitches before I get an assignment," you're going to smile if number 50 is a hit. If you go in there thinking every pitch is going to land you an assignment, you're going to be in for a disastrous ego pop. It's really a numbers game; it's like dating, it's like sales, it's like anything that requires massive amounts of follow-through, follow-up, diligence, continuous belief in yourself.

I freelanced for about eight years. I had the best time because you could write off everything. You got to go to free appointments, free events. Everything could be a story, so every single person you met became of interest to you in some way. It was this exciting search of clips, clips, clips. Everything you do becomes confirmation and affirmation of who you are as a writer. That's when things are going well.

And then you are challenged when you get bad feedback from an editor, or no feedback, or someone rejects [your pitch]. Or a piece you were counting on for money comes back, and they say they aren't running it and they aren't even giving you a kill fee [what a publication pays you if they don't end up running an article they assigned]. That's when it becomes really hard. That's why you never go into this business without having a backup source of money. Whether it's a bartending job or whatever. I always had one steady client paying the bills, giving me like $2,000 a month. Or two steady clients. I was hustling, and everything on top of that was like gravy.

I was in an office with a secretary, but I felt lonely . . . because I wasn't around people who . . . [were] doing things that I found inspiring. I was around drones.

Another good way to break in is obviously getting a beginning job as an editorial assistant at a magazine. That really helps you because it gives you connections, which are very helpful in getting your stuff read. I worked as an editorial assistant at *Working Woman Magazine*. That was my first job in magazines. It was really scary.

Prior to that I was working in advertising, and I was miserable in the advertising business because I just felt so completely lonely—and I was in an office with a secretary—but I felt lonely. Why? Because I wasn't around people who meant something to me, [were] doing things that I found inspiring. I was around drones. So I moved to a new neighborhood on a whim. And before I knew it, I wanted to quit my job and start working for a magazine. Because I was inspired by the people. Here were these fantastic people struggling next to me, doing what I wanted to do, and now were just one step ahead of me, saying I could get there, I could get there. I needed to be inspired.

I was leaving a secretary behind in order to be a virtual secretary to someone else. I had worked my way up; I was making pretty good money. And I left it all and took a several-thousand-dollar pay cut in order to do this crazy job of being someone's secretary. And the editor of *Working Woman* said, "We really didn't want to hire you because we think you're crazy!" But I was so determined to be a writer.

Jonathan Ames on Becoming a Novelist

Jonathan Ames is the author of I Pass Like Night, The Extra Man, What's Not to Love?, My Less Than Secret Life, *and* Wake Up, Sir! *He is the winner of a Guggenheim Fellowship and a former columnist for the* New York Press. *Mr. Ames contributes to the radio show* The Next Big Thing *and is a recurring guest on the* Late Show with David Letterman.

I always tell aspiring novelists that there will be more rejection than acceptance. I tell them some of the things I went through. I'd written and published a novel by the time I was 25, and then for a few years I tried to kind of force myself to write a book, just because I thought I had to be published again.

Then I had a class with the writer Richard Price, and he said that he went through that—that he felt like a good dog when published and a bad dog when not published—and that he had sort of written a book just to be published. The book was no good, so he realized that he had to find something he was in love with to write about. I realized I had to get back to my roots of writing—why I love to write—and not just because I wanted to be published.

Mimicry and stealing, you know, every great writer does that. You end up putting things through your own filter, through your own psyche.

I ended up speaking to Richard Price [whose novel *Samaritan* follows a police detective] afterwards, and he offered to give me the number of a police detective in Jersey City. [Observing that world had] actually turned around his writing career because he so loved the scene, the dialogue, and the characters. So I realized I had to find something I was in love with to write about. I didn't end up calling [the detective], but I found a world that I wanted to hang out in. This was back in '92, and I just moved to New York and I had started grad school. I mean, I had published a novel, went through an MFA program because a friend of mine said, "As long as you're in school, you're not failing. . . "

The MFA program was a good decision for me because I was driving a taxi, and now I had time to write. It was a good decision; mostly it was just to have time and deadlines, stuff like that.

So I took Richard Price's advice and tried to find things I was in love with, so I would tell young writers that. I also tell them to write the kind of stories that they like to read. I tell them to mimic the authors they love. Mimicry and stealing, you know, every great writer does that. You end up putting things through your own filter, through your own psyche. Look at James Joyce; he mimicked *The Odyssey*. Using that structure gave him a vessel through which to pour the stories he wanted to tell.

I did have a lot of debt after the MFA program, and I always tell people to go to MFA programs where you get scholarships and where you teach to pay for your classes. It's very dangerous to be a writer and have debt. I always tell young people to not go to an expensive MFA program, but to go to the ones where you can get a scholarship.

It's not easy, getting grants, but it's worth doing. You can find everything you want to know about the writing game in *Poets & Writers* magazine.

I also tell young writers to go back and study their grammar a little. I'm not kidding. I had a huge change in my ability to write when I started teaching composition courses at the business school, and by having to teach grammar, it rooted me back in the sentence and cleared up anything that I had been secretly confused about for years.

The basic structure of the sentence—I didn't fully get it. I had been taught grammar in sixth or seventh grade and my brain didn't absorb it back then. Then as a 30-year-old person, I got it. Subject, verb—I don't know—it just gave me better control of the sentence. So I often tell young writers to go pick up the composition book and just spend a day looking at the grammar stuff. It's kind of like the scales on the piano.

Simon Foster on Writing That Actually Pays Money

Hot shot. Australian. Has an accent. Simon has worked for clients like IBM, *Kodak, Volkswagon, and Toyota in print, radio,* TV, *and web-based mediums. Currently with Ogilvy in New York, he started his career at the similarly high-flying agency Saatchi & Saatchi in Sydney.*

Copywriting, a lot of the time, is writing a list in a way so that it doesn't sound like it's a list. It's kind of like a creative process. You're just trying to write something that tells people a whole bunch of things without boring them to death [while] getting them interested in the whole thing. There are lots of people around the world trying to say that their cars are cleaner than everyone else's, so the way to kind of make it impact on consumers is to express that in a way that they aren't expecting so that they'll remember. Basically, we're paid to come up with interesting ways to say things. For example, for an environmentally friendly car, one ad I did showed the back of the car and the muffler or the exhaust pipe was shaped like a heart, and the headline said, "No other car is kinder to the planet." It's an interesting job.

I actually have a degree in writing, so I do write fiction and stuff. But one thing I've found with advertising is that it's hard to try to keep your private creative interests going when you work in advertising. . .

It sucks up a lot of your time and a lot of your creative energy—but I think that's the price you have to pay. You expend so much thought in the creative area of advertising, to come home and want to do that on your own, it's hard. I find it hard, anyway. I think a lot of people do. It's easy to just go have a few beers and shut down for a while, rather than to keep pushing yourself creatively. But having said that, it is really well paid, and it's interesting work.

As a copywriter, you work with an art director, and someone might come to you and say, "We want to do an ad for a car." You work in teams. Some teams sit there and concentrate [on] ideas. I prefer to work by myself, then get together with the other person and say, "Look, what have you got?" and then kind of see where it goes. Everyone approaches it really differently, and everyone kind of has their own idea about what a good ad is. Across the industry, there's no real consensus. So when we're given a brief like that, at that stage, the copywriter and the art director don't really take different roles. They just generate ideas.

Once we've generated a bunch of ideas, they kind of go through the internal mechanism between the agent and

Copywriting, a lot of the time, is writing a list in a way so that it doesn't sound like it's a list.

the client. And when a client actually buys an ad, that's when we split up more. The writer will go and write the copy and do all of that, and the art director will go away and make sure that the ad is shot properly. That's basically how my job works.

When you first start, you really can drive yourself crazy because you can think about the work all the time if you want to. I think that when you first get into the industry, you're a little paranoid that you're never going to come up with a decent solution to a brief, and so you do think about it all the time. I think that's counterproductive. After you've been doing it for a while, you realize you have to just forget about it over the weekends and when you go home and stuff. It can get a little too all-consuming sometimes, I think.

All of the creatives [industry term for copywriters and art directors, as opposed to those on the business side, who are called "account people"] I know in America got into the industry by going to ad school. There are ad schools around the country where you pay $20,000 or $25,000 a year to go [to] these ad schools and get taught to write ads. Then you come out of there, and because these ad schools have connections with agencies, they line up days where people from agencies come and look at [the portfolios] of all the students, and the agencies pick the good ones. And that's how people get in. In New York, a lot of people go to the School of Visual Arts. Then there are places like the Ad School in Miami, and the Creative Circus in Atlanta.

Try to talk to some people who work in agencies before you embark on one of these courses. Talk to some people in advertising to figure out whether or not it's for you because it is demanding and stressful. Basically what I did was, I went to

[a] headhunter in Sydney and I got a whole list of names off of him of who the best creatives were in Sydney.

Then I just started going to see them, which is kind of a hard thing to do. I just started ringing them up and saying, "Can I come see you and show you my work?" You've at least got to do some work so you've got something to show them. I'd go to them and say, "Look, I've done this." And they'd go, "Yeah, it's OK, but it's kind of not good enough to get a job." And I'd say, "Well, give me a brief on something. What are you guys working on? Can you give me a brief that you've got, and I'll go and do some work on it and come back with it?" Some people would say OK. You'd go in and do some ads, and come back about a month later and show them.

I did that for a few months, and then I met guy at [the ad agency] Saatchi & Saatchi in Sydney that kind of liked me. He's like, "Your book's OK, but to get into the industry, it has to be fantastic. But what if I give you a brief each week and you fax me work every Wednesday? I want to see all the work you're doing, not just what's in your book." So I started doing that with him, and that really elevated the standard of my work really quickly, just because he took me seriously and it made me work more. Eventually out of that I got some freelance work at Saatchi.

Starting salaries are very low because it's so hard to break into advertising. So the agencies kind of exploit that because they know you really want to work there. That's kind of the price you have to pay in a way; you kind of have to be a slave for six months or something until you get enough good work shown, and they'll either put you on full-time or someone else will be interested [in you].

If you go to one of those ad schools in the U.S., then I think they'll have a whole process to help you get your portfolio together so that it looks professional. But there's nothing wrong with just doing it yourself. I'm a copywriter and I can't really draw, but the book I was showing people was kind of my drawing basically. That really doesn't matter that much. It's more the idea. But obviously, the better you can finish things, the better it is. People are really more interested in the ideas anyway. People in advertising move around a lot, so you have to keep your book and yourself marketable. That's what people will want.

What to Do Now, aka the Final Pep Talk

A friend of mine was recently talking to a woman he was interested in having sex with about what the term *success* means in America. It's a topic worth meditating on, but perhaps one you'd only discuss out loud if you were engaged in a sort of pre-tantric dance such as this one. This woman or love object's contention was that Americans immediately think of professional accomplishments when faced with the term. (The reason she speaks of Americans in the third person, just for the record, is that she lived in France for a year.) In France, she said, success is a measure of one's personal life, one's love life and the robustness of one's friendships, chiefly. Apparently, I am typically American in this regard. Success does make me think of careers, as those other categories seem tied to happiness. I ask my friend what he thinks and he says, with trademark goofiness, "That's

People don't become big successes pursuing careers they feel ambivalent about.

what she said, man. But I don't know. I've never been to France."

I bring up this anecdote, about people and their units of measure (which also makes me wonder if he arrived at Success that night) because this is something you're going to want to determine for yourself. DJ AM said his mom always equated success with happiness, and, not for nothing, his career is a model for both. He was working in a mailroom when he got his first resident DJ gig at a hip club in Los Angeles. And now, years later and with scads of celebrity parties under his belt (and a beautiful fiancée in Nicole Ritchie) one of his most marked characteristics—besides a deep, deep voice—is gratitude. It's also a quality many of the aspiring DJs he knows seem to lack.

As for other leitmotifs, I can hardly believe how many of the success stories here are functions of patience and persistence. Jewelry designer Melissa Joy Manning was, for a good long while, hanging by a thread and taking business classes before she became a darling of Barneys. It took director Jesse Peretz five years to get the green light to make his first feature film, and six years for Jean-Georges to come up with his own great recipes. Only after enduring "bringer" shows did comedian Eric Drysdale discover an alternate route in which to hone his writing and his standup talents that didn't bankrupt his friends.

The same goes for musician Chris Conley, who holds life on his tour bus in particularly high regard because he and his bandmates were used to sleeping on cat-vomit-covered basement floors. Each and all of these examples only serves to underscore the fact that people don't become big successes pursuing careers they feel ambivalent about.

Regardless of profession, from here on out you must be an entrepreneur.

There are also some insidious consequences to the fact that our American, ahem, society reveres youth over the experienced. The flip side of youth worship, of course, is that there's commensurately more pressure to achieve greatness at a young age. "Last hired, first fired" is certainly an employment guideline that no longer holds. Most companies would rather hire two hungry employees than keep on another vice president. And, to wit, we might not even be that hungry anymore. We've marginalized the older people, which wouldn't necessarily be so bad except that we destroy our bosses and mentors in the process. So instead of a roadmap, or a career guide to fabulousness, we see Weekend Warriors and bloated Bernie Ebbers types we would never wish to emulate. Not only that, but loyalty has become a middle-aged value.

God, how depressing. But fear not, friends. What all this means is that, regardless of profession, from here on out you must be an entrepreneur. Look to people like Heatherette—two nocturnal talents with a penchant for glitter, or Jeff Shesol, a writer who was hand-scouted by President Clinton—for cues to whether or not you're on the right path. Know your value in the marketplace, as well as how to negotiate. Package yourself wisely—not like bargain-brand cereal but cleverly, like Altoids. Or Jason West. And pay particular attention to Jessica Naddaff's invaluable advice on how to be your own publicist, which is a useful skill set to have and know no matter what your career path—especially if your field of choice is a creative one.

I am hoping that you will find instant and lasting achievement in whatever field you choose to pursue. And that the pursuit of such dreams will not involve a bed made of asphalt. But even if it does, promise me you won't let yourself get hung up on comparisons. Because in addition to there always being someone younger and more successful around to devil you, there will also always be someone who has more connections, too. Or is, for instance, named Coppola.

Now, I could cheerlead and coo at you for ages yet, and I'd like to, but you have some phone calls to make. You have so much information here at your fingertips. So, for now, go forth, and be very, very brave.

About the Author

Katy McColl, Senior Editor/ Writer for JANE magazine, joined its staff in 2000 and currently writes monthly feature columns on various aspects of American culture. These topics range from modern etiquette to multimillion dollar modeling scams. She has also written about a double homicide on an Indian reservation in Montana and gone undercover to report on family dynamics in illegal polygamous societies.

Prior to her position with JANE, McColl worked on the launch of Vogue.com/Style.com and at *Travel + Leisure*. She co-authored *Lonely Planet's 2004 Guide to New York City*. McColl graduated from Smith College in 1999 with a Bachelor's degree in Spanish literature. While in college, she taught Spanish to elementary school kids and was awarded the English department's prize for best fiction.

When not working, this Dallas, Texas, native enjoys reading old novels and new non-fiction and often travels to small towns in search of used books and vintage dresses. She lives in Brooklyn, New York.